Gary Brewer

ELOQUENT EYE

Studio Visits with Artists of Los Angeles

2017 - 2023

GRIFFITH MOON Los Angeles

IVA GUEORGUIEVA

PAUL PAIEMENT

SIMPHIWE NDZUBE

REBECCA FARR

ALISON SAAR

TIM HAWKINSON

KATHERINA OLSCHBAUR

KIMBERLY BROOKS

NASIM HANTEHZADEH

MERCEDES DORAME

FORREST KIRK

UMAR RASHID

MATTHEW BRANDT

ELLIOTT HUNDLEY

Gary Brewer

ELOQUENT EYE

Studio Visits with Artists of Los Angeles

2017 – 2023

With a foreword by

Janelle Zara

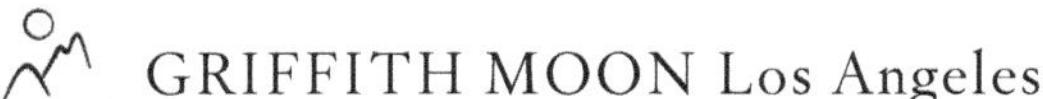 GRIFFITH MOON Los Angeles

ISBN: 978-1-7367738-4-0
Library of Congress Control Number: 2024945936

The following essays are reprinted by permission from
Hyperallergic, Alison Saar "I Wanted to Make Art That Told a Story"
May 2018, *Whitehot Magazine*, Matthew Brandt "Light & Matter"
May 2022, Elliott Hundley "Echo" March 2023, and all other
interviews, *Art and Cake Magazine*, 2017 - 2021.

Cover Design by Heather Sue Tokarsky
Book Layout and Typesetting by Heather Sue Tokarsky
Cover Detail *Sisters*, oil on linen, 2021 by Katherina Olschbaur
First Printing, 2024

All photos by Gary Brewer except for Kimberly Brooks, photo
credit Stebs Schinnerer, and Gary Brewer, photo credit Aline Mare.

Published by Griffith Moon
Los Angeles, California
www.GriffithMoon.com

Contents

Tip the world over on its side and everything loose will land in Los Angeles.

> Frank Lloyd Wright, *Frank Lloyd Wright on Architecture, Nature, and the Human Spirit: A Collection of Quotations*

Preface

The world indeed has been upended. A seismic shift has realigned the magnetic poles, and the art world is seeing a shift in the nexus where the planet's creative souls converge.

Many factors make Los Angeles an ideal city to nurture a contemporary zeitgeist. It has long been criticized as a vapid, glittering mirage, a phenomenon of impermanence that grew rapidly without a plan or design, a hodgepodge of communities linked by a nightmarish gnarl of freeways. Greater Los Angeles is indeed a Byzantine sprawl of cities. The world has filled this crazy urban quilt with a rich weave of cultures, and these cultures are synthesizing new language forms with images and metaphors that tell human-scale stories the world is hungry to hear.

There has been an enormous divide between the world of the visual arts and the world at large. For decades, a cynical, irony-laden smog has filled the language of much of the contemporary art world. It has obscured the sunlight of metaphor and meaning and spawned an inbred genre of "art about art," using tight philosophical and linguistic knots to squeeze out some semblance of meaning. This has created a cultural fissure between a wider audience and the visual arts: a closing of the windows and drawing of the blinds.

In the last decade, the Western canon of art history has been shattered, and the resulting cracks have let in the light. Women and artists of color who had been excluded from the conversation have entered the room, and the party has taken on a delightful, much more gregarious tone. Every museum in major cities is frantically diving into its storage racks and brushing off decades of dust to bring to light artists whose work adds a vital and powerful contribution to the story of our world.

The number of artists from all walks of life getting their time in the sun has exploded, and the world is so much richer for it. Storytelling in novel imagistic forms and the use of materials that convey the history of a people and the sociopolitical forces that have shaped their world are opening up fresh avenues of expression.

A decentralized, nebulous shape-shifting landscape, i.e., a city without a center, is more conducive to the cultural dynamics of our contemporary world. Planned cities like New York that fashioned themselves on a European model are less nimble and fluid than the strange hybridized, unstructured growth of Los Angeles, with its never-ending kaleidoscope of communities and cultures. This is a historical shift: the Los Angeles zeitgeist now comparable to the energy and excitement in the art world of Paris in the 1920s or New York in the 1950s.

One might add that the geological forces of Southern California bring a dramatic note to the city. We live in a subduction zone, where tectonic plates converge beneath the earth on which we stand. The precarity and existential power of this dynamic is another layer of myth and metaphor that imbues the region's aura. The rise and fall of mountains, cities, and civilizations are written in the geological forces at play: the San Gabriel Mountains to the north of downtown LA are among the fastest-growing mountains in the world. Pressure from the San Andreas Fault to the north and a series of thrust faults on their south face cause them to grow as much as two inches a year.

This rapid growth and dynamic change in geology is reflected in the mercurial nature of the art world. Springs of creativity well up from the deep aquifer of talent that has found space in this parched landscape. A desert only in name, this land of sun and sea has become a new shimmering star of the 21st century international artistic community. What was once seen as a negative trait—the chimerical and impermanent nature of Los Angeles, a city where the center does not hold—has become an asset; the nimbleness and fluid nature of its vastness has produced a cultural ecosystem of endless possibilities.

This book is a historical record from 2017 to 2023; the essays are organized in order of the years in which they were written.

The following chapters are a record of some of the artists whose creativity is rooted and flowering within the dynamism of this protean cultural landscape: today's Los Angeles.

I often think that many of the works that are canonically labeled "great" are simply those that lingered longest in individual memory. And that they lingered because while looking at them someone was moved, touched, taken to another place, momentarily born again.
Bell Hooks, 1993

The one thing to say about art is that it is one thing. Art is art-as-art and everything else is everything else.
Ad Reinhardt, 1962

Foreword by
Janelle Zara

When examining what makes an artist tick, the perspective of another artist provides a unique alternative to that of a critic or art historian alone. The questions and line of inquiry are cast with a more personal and curious hue and the resulting repartee lays bare details that might otherwise go unnoticed. Enter writer-artist Gary Brewer, who has engaged and curated a group of Los Angeles artists in their natural habitat. As the center of gravity of the art world moves westward, this combination of essays offers a beautiful snapshot of what is happening right now in the first quarter of the 21st century on the West Coast of America. Each essay describes a studio visit with a Los Angeles artist—an in-depth encounter that always begins with one question: "What, as an artist, are you trying to do?" What ensues between the artist and the writer is a collaborative unpacking, less interview than conversation. Together they locate different elements of the artist's practice within a larger but intimately personal worldview, stretching beyond the parameters of art into myriad other topics: mythology, music, world history, religion, Simphiwe Ndzube's childhood in Cape Town building furniture and toy cars out of mud and scraps of wire, Iva Gueorguieva's reading of Rebecca Solnit in terms of space, landscape and city. These are the many points of reference that artists, like all of us, use to build out a framework through which they understand the world which in turn molds the contours of their art.

This understanding of art—as a physical and philosophical extension of the artist—is where worldview and aesthetic combine. Artistic practice satisfies a very specific compulsion—to repeatedly lean the entirety of one's being into a medium, then bare the resulting physical impression before the world. We find evidence of this in the writer's studio visit with Tim Hawkinson, where layers of latex that the artist had painted onto his naked body had dried into a second skin; this replica of the self made it possible for Hawkinson to explore the parts of his own body which had always been hidden from him. Physically and philosophically, the piece embodies Brewer's description of the artistic process as the "poetic inquiry into the unknown."

Art is what the artist retrieves beyond the walls of the familiar: "a methodology for mapping the contours of what is just out of reach, around the corner from cognition."

Brewer does not record his studio visits. He simply listens intently and processes information in real time to gain deeper insights through empathy, a mode of momentarily inhabiting the palace of the artist's mind and looking at their work through their own eyes. As Elliott Hundley makes reference to the works of Euripides, Rilke, and others, Brewer cites these influences in the phantasmagoria of the artist's work. He describes Hundley's explosive collages, comprising thousands of elaborately composed, miniscule cutouts, as "myths and stories … representative of states of consciousness," where maximalist excess reflects the overwhelming complexity of living. "The stories and the characters in them are not only a method to give subjective shape to his work, but … archetypal actors from our collective unconscious who have helped Hundley create his sense of identity."

Brewer's uncanny work—identifying various compositional choices and tracing them back to their origins in the brain—treats art itself as a composite of disparate elements of our being. Truly seeing a work of art is recognizing the artist for exactly who they are. This is the poet's approach to reading a work of art: seeking out the poetry in others.

Janelle Zara, Critic
Los Angeles, 2024

What I seek is a permanent opening of possibilities.
Michel Foucault, *The Foucault Reader*

Leave the door open for the unknown, the door into the dark. That's where the most important things come from, where you yourself came from, and where you will go.
Rebecca Solnit, *A Field Guide to Getting Lost*

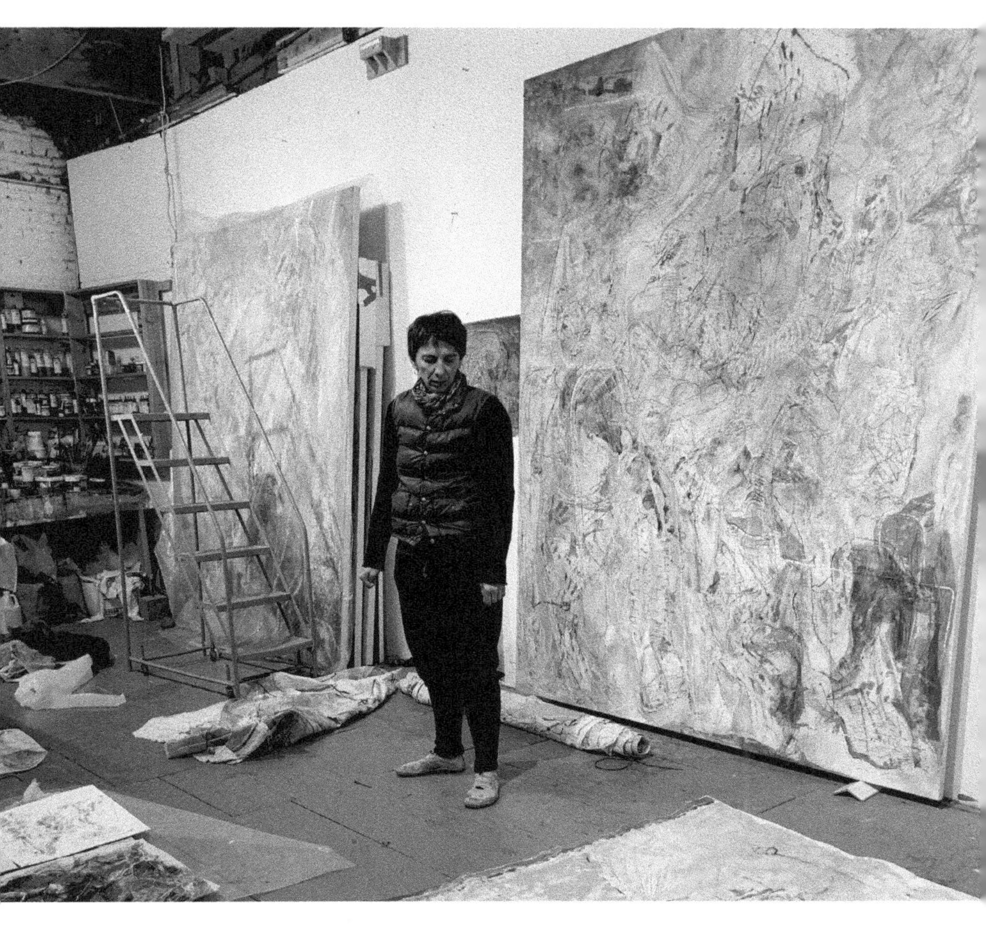

IVA GUEORGUIEVA

A Translator of the Senses

I va Gueorguieva tells stories, or better, stories are told through her. Her "memory body" filters the myriad narratives that she encounters and that saturate her consciousness. She has an acute memory, collecting observations from the books she reads and the world at large: random bits of information, a person's face, their expression, their posture, the room in which she saw them, fragments of life's living theater collected like colorful pieces of fabric. Then she unfurls these memories and ideas onto her vast canvases, weaving them together improvisationally to inform the metanarratives that emerge in her large-scale "abstractions."

> *I do not paint images, the paintings are improvisational. I bring everything from my life experience and knowledge to the work. I set up limitations to create within. It's a way to frame the work, to guide it into an area of interest, a subject emerges within these constraints.*

Though her paintings are "abstract," she uses abstraction as a way to give herself the freedom to invent form—they accommodate all the episodic references that flow from her hand, from her body. Out of the complexity of her gestural-architectonic weave, appearing from this rich sea of cross-referencing elements, a "figure" may emerge. In fact, she spoke of her process as a sort of subjective roaming: to lose oneself is to discover something new, to see things anew.

We spoke of the writer Rebecca Solnit, whose work we both love, of her ability to show us that the images we know of the landscape, of the city, are never neutral, but framed by ideas and systems that inform our perception of them. Gueorguieva spoke of the way Solnit's writings explore a "space," and from that investigation a "figure" emerges, a figure from history, maybe. The way Solnit's investigations lead organically to this emergence in some ways parallels Gueorguieva's approach to painting.

The idea of the city is important to her work: it is a system and a metaphor of political power and desire.

The city, she said, *is a place of power where flesh and the machine meet, where bodies close together in these air-conditioned spaces procreate. Cities are an organism, a system of power, the heart of power.*

Her paintings are crowded, filled with many elements, subjective players that converse in crowd scenes of desire.

Gueorguieva told me she thought of cities as organisms and that she wanted to reshape them, to stack them and compress them, sweeping them together into different forms. We spoke about the architectonic quality of her work, how some of the "abstract" paintings I had seen in past exhibits oscillated between a flat allover abstraction and passages that had spatial depth, creating a hidden pressure, the ambiguity translating into a kind of subjective compression. In addition to her paintings, Gueorguieva makes sculptures that are independent works in themselves, but also a way for her to feel the spaces that she invents, to climb inside the architectural forms of her paintings and embed those spatial feelings into her body. They are experiential objects whose making informs and shapes her "body memory." When she paints, the sensation of this spatial depth is part of her: in fluid improvisations physical memories emerge, another element in this rich space of untethered subjective dialogue.

The artist brings all of her experience to her paintings—what she is reading, a fragment of a story or a memory, something that moved her and embedded itself in her soul. She showed me a painting with loosely applied gestural strokes of yellow filling the central area; strips of red material had been glued to the surface, creating a feeling of movement and light. She said the piece was a reference to a road trip she took many years ago. She and her husband stopped their car in the desert and saw an abandoned silo off a short distance. As Iva walked toward it, an enormous white owl flew out, sweeping past her. She continued walking, entered the vast space, and inside it another white owl was flying in circles, slowly ascending toward the light to escape through an opening at the top. It was one of the most beautiful things she had ever seen, and she was trying to capture something of it in this painting.

Toward the end of our conversation she mentioned that she felt her impulse toward storytelling came partly from her Bulgarian heritage, that it is ingrained in her DNA to infuse her visual gestures with narratives. Gueorguieva pointed out a painting with a figure of a woman, a witch bending down, her body a compilation of fragments, gestural strokes in blacks, reds and turquoise, a kind of "stenographic figure" within a swirling field of forms. She told me that historically, in Bulgaria it was the women's task to go to the mountain spring to collect water. It was a place of danger as well as a source of life. One could be bitten by a snake or abducted by someone or by some evil force. It was a place for storytelling and a place where stories originated.

Gueorguieva's paintings are like a river of ideas, their movement reshaping the landscape around us. Her art is a place where the dynamics of memory, ideas, images and primal forces are transmuted into visual dramas. She is a translator of the senses, with sound, taste, touch and smell becoming visual experience. Her paintings contain the sensation of desire, the aspiration to transpose all of life, power, love and death into her work to convey the mortal weight of time.

Through the process of coevolution human ideas find their way into natural facts. ... The offspring of the ancient marriage of plants and people are far stranger and more marvelous than we realize.
Michael Pollan, *The Botany of Desire*

"Cartesian space" had a physical dimensionality.
... Perspective ... fit perfectly into this rationalized model of space.
Anne Friedberg, *The Virtual Window: From Alberti to Microsoft*

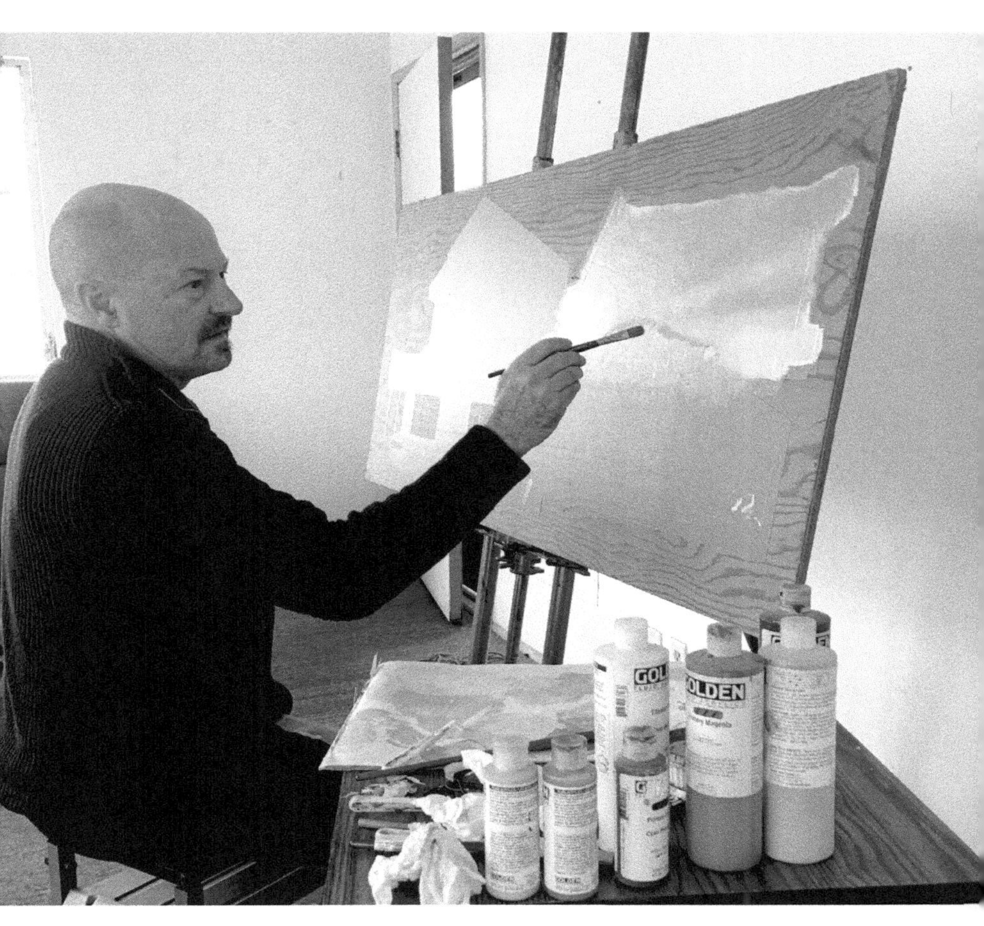

PAUL PAIEMENT

*Synthetic Hybrid
Spirituality*

Reconciliation is a form of spiritual practice: to reconcile opposites, differences and perceptions. For Paul Paiement it is a philosophical conundrum from which his visual language arises. Paiement's paintings hybridize the "man-made" synthetic elements of "culture" with the natural world; his deeply felt images explore the space between those two worlds and visualize them as part of the same natural order.

Despite our seeming separation from nature, we are very much indeed "nature." Humans are animals whose needs for survival, relationships, love and beauty define our activities, our language, our inventions and the buildings and cities we design. But at the same time, our perceptions define the way that we interpret information, and our thoughts shape those perceptions. Single-point perspective is an invention, a way to order our senses and to perceive the world in a specific way, one that matches the utilitarian and purpose-driven design of our buildings and roads. It enforces the Cartesian impulse of the rational mind seeking order in place of the perceived "chaos" of nature.

When I visited Paiement in his studio, he was spending countless hours on beautiful paintings of landscapes from locations he had captured in photographs, sublime images that suggest the Romanticism of Caspar David Friedrich. They are composed and crafted with the deep love of a painter who is passionate about painting, about touch and materials. On top of these he places silhouettes of buildings, finely cut out in colored and clear plexiglass. The interplay of the transparent overlay with the open areas where the paintings are left unobscured is finely balanced, the play of the architectonic shapes in perspective against the Romantic landscapes carefully composed. Of these works, Paiement says,

I feel we are living in a time similar to the Romantic generation. Their impulse was inspired by, and a response to, the rapid changes of the industrial revolution. Those poets and painters—Emerson, Caspar David Friedrich, the Hudson River Valley School—were seeking a rebuke to the modernization of life. We live in a similar time, where so much change is occurring at such a high rate of speed that there is a similar impulse to look to nature. We are in the middle of something and we do not know where it is going. It is an exciting time to be alive.

In his paintings he seeks to reconcile the landscape and its natural order of elemental forces producing the irregularities of the mountains, valleys and meadows, with the logical perspective of human-made structures, buildings, homes and spaces—the constructs of "human nature" in balance within nature. They are poetic metaphors about our innate need to create spaces to inhabit within the natural forces around us, of how we shape nature to suit our needs, and the idea that nature may interact with us to promote its needs. In Michael Pollan's *Botany of Desire*, the author makes a fascinating case for the idea of co-evolution, and in some ways Paiement's paintings touch upon this concept.

These paintings are not political in nature, though Paiement says,

If someone sees it that way, run with it, it is yours to use as you wish.

He believes that if metaphors are deep enough and true enough, they will have the space to encompass varying interpretations, that they "contain multitudes." In my mind these are optimistic paintings, they celebrate the brilliance of nature, culture and human invention. Rather than stopping the clock and going back to some musing about an anterior "golden age," these paintings assert a radiance and joy in both nature and human nature. In his insect paintings the joy is palpable, smart and elegant. The colorful permutations and juxtapositions of natural shapes against manufactured forms embody a delightful interspecies dialogue. They celebrate both the "natural" and "cultural" inventions of form.

There is a spiritual aspect to these architectural silhouettes superimposed on the natural world, and to his paintings of insects where the natural and synthetic fuse. As Paiement put it,

It is an assertion of an existential fact that we live here, that no matter how hard we try, we leave our footprint on this Earth and that we have to acknowledge that, to accept this reality as it simply is.

In Paiement's universe these things co-exist as facts, neither good nor bad: they simply are. His paintings seek to reconcile these seemingly different worlds into poetic hybrids where natural forms morph into synthetic ones, where the space within a natural setting is complemented by the rectilinear silhouette of a building in which the single-point perspective is not a contradiction or a conqueror, but another aspect of "nature," of our "human nature." Our minds have created the formal logic of rectilinear design for function, and that has its place in the natural order of things as much as the geometry of ripples emanating from a pebble dropped into a pond. There is an almost Buddhist perspicacity in this acceptance of things as they are, that these seeming opposites are in fact a part of the same "whole."

"Noun and verb, abstraction and representation": these are words and concepts whose meanings are interchangeable. It is the dialogue between these interchangeable worldviews that Paiement explores in his paintings, installations and ceramic sculptures. These philosophical and conceptual musings could be words without meaning, but in the hands, eye and mind of Paul Paiement the ideas are reconciled in psychologically complex paintings. His sense of design is exquisite, the transitional zones where an insect's body morphs into some man-made element, a smart car or a helicopter, are metaphorically rich. His paintings are serious philosophical assertions, deeply satisfying and at times playful and eccentric, but always with a very high level of craft fusing dialogues between abstraction and representation into deeply resolved works of art.

Painting is a language whose internal logic is a forceful communicator of ideas. It has a conviction and power that makes philosophical ideas a physical fact. The facts are metaphors, nimble enough to adapt to changing times and perceptions. In these paintings Paiement muses something that is relevant now and will be relevant far into the future: how do we see clearly, how can we understand the world, nature and our innate needs? In Paiement's worldview it is an exciting time to be alive and to engage deeply with life in all its permutations.

If a man has his eyes bound, you can encourage him as much as you like to stare through the bandage, but he will never see anything. Illusions are more common than changes in fortune.
Franz Kafka, *The Castle*

How thin and insecure is that little beach of white sand we call consciousness. I've always known that in my writing it is the dark troubled sea of which I know nothing, save its presence, that carried me. I've always felt that creating was a fearless and a timid, a despairing and hopeful, launching out into that unknown.
Athol Fugard, *Notebooks 1960/1977*

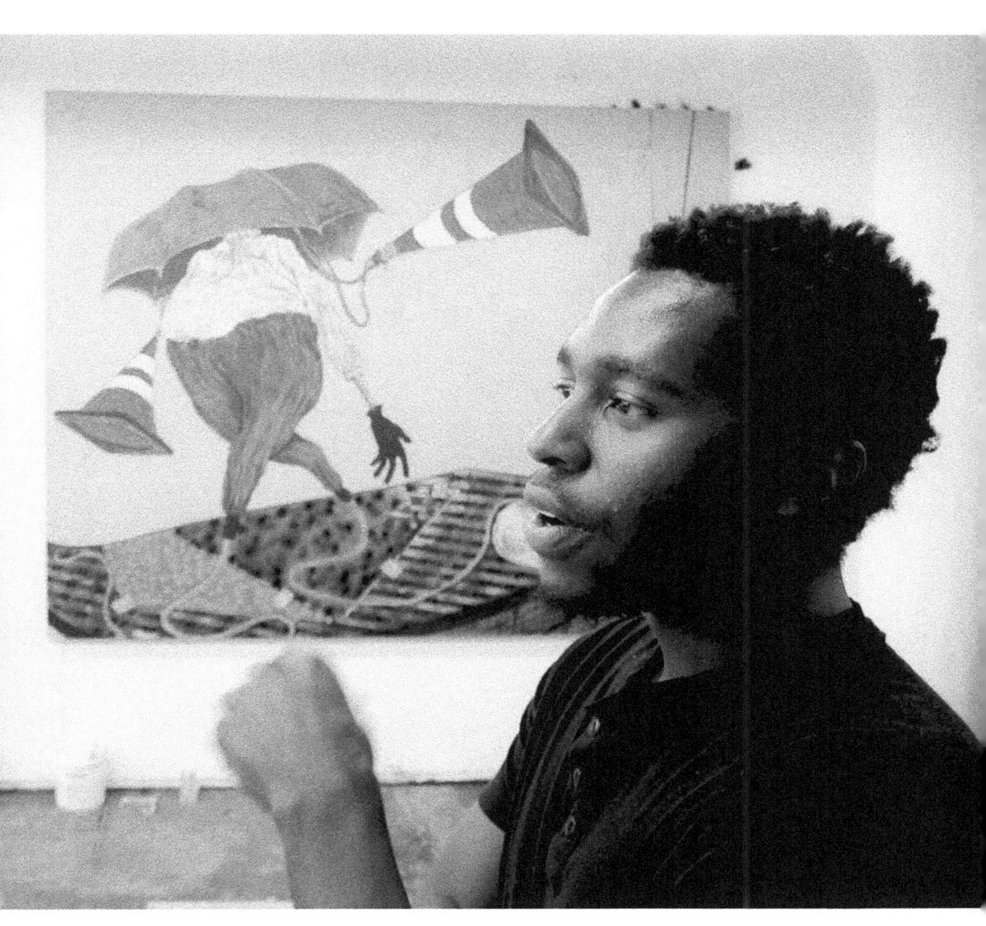

SIMPHIWE NDZUBE

A Journey Through the Theater of the Absurd

Through metaphor and myth we seek to express themes that speak not to the particulars of a time and place but to the conditions of life in universal terms: it is a need to depict the everyman and everywoman as players in this tragicomedy of life. From the tarot deck, the fool steps off a cliff, his eyes bright, looking with certainty at the horizon to begin his journey. Two vaudevillians wait in an empty landscape for the all-knowing Godot to give meaning to the absurdity of the emptiness that envelop them. Lady Macbeth cannot cleanse her hands of the blood from the primal murder—absolution is not possible for this grim deed. These images speak to us outside of time, race, and gender; they reach into the heart of the matter—the heart of darkness, of our communion with oblivion—the dance of life performed against the void.

Bhabharosi is a figure from a mythic realm that Simphiwe Ndzube has created. "Bhabha" comes from the word "barbarous," meaning "uncivilized; wild; savage; crude"; "rosi" is Ndzube's addition, creating an improvised language representing this alternate universe where the "fool's journey" is unfolding. Bhabharosi climbs and jumps, falls and stumbles through a netherworld that is a theater composed of random bits of the world we know. Some elements contain a narrative intent, a car or a boat for transport to reach the other shore; others are the things Ndzube may see walking to his studio in DTLA. His works have a playful spontaneity grounded by a sinister undercurrent that infuses the environments with a feeling of disquiet; a sense of foreboding pervades the spaces that his figures journey through.

The paintings are large, the paint applied loosely with richly worked surfaces. There are passages with strident patterns created using both brush and paint from spray cans; their striking colors generate an optical energy in the images. Lavender is a dominant color recurring as the backdrop to these wildly haphazard compositions. They teeter and collapse as the figures scurry and dance through the stark stage sets of this fleeting world. Headless, their legs become whips, dangerous tools of pain, and simultaneously turn into tentacles reaching and grabbing, climbing, exploring the world. In many paintings Ndzube adds stuffed clothes, pants and shirts whose appendages end in knots, sometimes ropes, that become whiplike extensions beyond the canvas.

The paintings freely move from image to object, and sculptural objects fill the studio as well. The sculptures have a lighter feel, the playfulness of the figures freed from the chromatically expressive force of his painted environments. Painted canvases on the floor create a ground for these sculptures; lights, fans, and umbrellas add an eccentric, circus-like atmosphere. Freed from the stark light within the paintings, Bhabharossi is dancing in the air, doing flips and somersaults.

Headless, genderless, and race-less Bhabharosi represents both everyman and everywoman, and also represents Ndzube himself embarking into an unknown world rich in possibilities but always within the existential facts on the ground: the capriciousness of fate, of who is born when and where, and of the unknown forces that shape our world and the circumstances we find ourselves in.

Ndzube was born in Cape Town, South Africa. As a child he and his siblings and friends would build small chairs and furnishings out of wood and mud; cars were made from wire, elaborate worlds were created including a hierarchy of status based on age. This was the early beginning of his life as a creative artist. Later, he and his friends found old thrown-out mattresses and piled them together to jump on and do flips. They also placed them under trees and would jump down doing somersaults; from this they developed skills that led to dance. From age 16 to 18 Ndzube was street dancing and thought he would become a professional dancer. But all the while he was drawing, creating images based on Japanese anime and other sources that he saw on television. When he was 13 he drew an elaborate anime character above his mother's bed.

When she came home, at first she was upset, but later realized that he was driven to create and bought him his first paints. He went on to attend the Michaelis School of Fine Art, one of the most prestigious schools on the continent.

He said of Cape Town and the world where he was raised, *There was an intensity that people put into everything that they did. Mainly involving extreme and dangerous activities that could end life in a snap. In the West there is an optimism that gives one a sense of luxury with time—in some parts of South Africa you knew you may not be here tomorrow, so everything was done with an intensity like it might be the last thing you do.*

As we spoke, I mentioned Beckett's *Waiting for Godot*, saying that the space the figures inhabited, with the cast-off refuse of the pedestrian world and the strange, barren light, felt like a stage set for Beckett. Ndzube smiled and said,

The title of this series is 'Waiting for Mlungu,' or 'Mungu,' a reference to the god of creation and bureaucracy, one who is remote and detached from man and living beings, in the beliefs of the Yao people of Mozambique and the Bantu people of sub-Saharan Africa. The word Mlungu was later altered to refer to white people as the dominant ruling class, and now it is used on the street among Black South Africans to mean that your are doing well financially, that you are making some money.

Ndzube is working on a series of screaming heads, a reference to Francis Bacon, whose work he loves. He said of these,

The scream in my paintings is something more than Bacon's existential terror, I want it to convey the burden of carrying the weight of this body in the world. I want the pressure of the world to force a different kind of air from the lungs of the screamer.

There is a haunting otherness to this world that the figures strive to understand, a world part Dr. Seuss inflected with Francis Bacon in a narrative drawn from Franz Kafka. Mlungu is an unattainable authority, one they will never reach, like "K" in Kafka's *The Castle*—there is no path that will take them to the authority they seek, just an endless labyrinth. Simultaneously, Bhabharosi expresses exuberance, a celebratory dance of life in which these figures, knowing the terms of their condition, are undeterred from their search.

Ndzube mentioned that while he was in school there was pressure on the Black South African students to focus on political realities, to make work that addressed the history of apartheid and the current racial tensions in their society. Of this Ndzube said,

> *It is a critical conversation that is needed as the majority of poor Black South Africans' lives remain harsh decades after the end of apartheid. But I felt that it was limiting me, I did not want my work to be temporal in nature, to speak about social conditions that would lose meaning in time. I wanted to speak in broader terms, in a way that was universal. I made Bhabharosi without race or gender so that it would speak for all people, not to entertain 'post-Black' or 'post-gender' ideas, but to make the figures I create travel through wider narratives. Bhabarosi's journey is on a mythic level and expresses the conditions of life that we want to escape, and the desire to re-create ourselves.*

These paintings in part represent his journey of rebellion and renewal, not to leave behind your origins, but to strive to create and explore one's potential and not be trapped within the arbitrary conditions of history and fate. On his own terms, Simphiwe Ndzube is exploring a mythic realm in which discovery and renewal are possible, but the weight and pressure of history will always be a factor shaping the outcome, forcing alternately a scream of despair and a cry of rejoicing.

Empathy makes you imagine the sensation of the torture, of the hunger, of the loss. You make that person into yourself, you inscribe their suffering on your body or heart or mind. ... Physical pain defines the physical boundaries of the self but these identifications define a larger self, a map of affections and alliances, and the limits of this psychic self are nothing more or less than the limits of love.
Rebecca Solnit, *The Faraway Nearby*

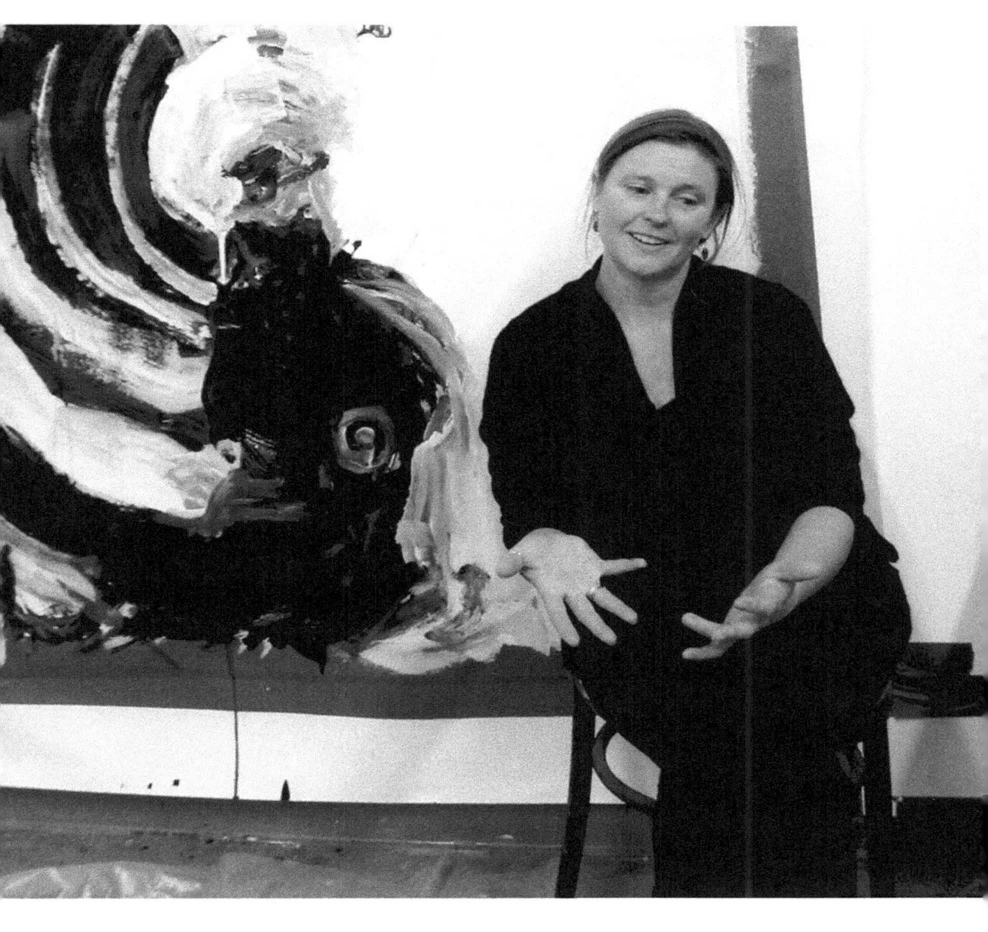

REBECCA FARR

*The Spiritual
Embodiment of Empathy*

Painting is a method to engage "self" in deep levels of cognition, beyond language and words. It is a space where somatic feelings and memories convey themselves outside of the conscious mind of the maker. They express aspects of the self by communicating through an immersive comprehension of thoughts and feelings. Rebecca Farr engages in works that seek to "embody" the spiritual and physical dimension of human suffering and, from this, to express a spiritual truth. They are paintings that use imagery culled from Goya, photographs from the Civil War, and early American photographic portraits. She allows the messy process of painting to dismantle the images; the immediacy of expression through color and touch comes to the fore, the images becoming ambiguous ciphers of human struggle. She seeks a moment of clarity: a *kenshō* experience through the murky uncertainty of painting. Rather than disengagement—using the light of the mind as a beacon to penetrate the source and cause of human suffering— she swims in the muddy waters, diving into the imprecision of memory and feeling to find a true reflection of this state of being. It is not in uncertain terms that Farr arrives at these metaphoric expressions; there is a clear moment of realization when the soul of her paintings makes itself known. It is spiritual in nature and touches something "divine" for Farr.

She said of her work and process,

I need to get lost in my work, in the process of painting. Destruction is an important part of the creative act; I will paint in and cover up areas again and again or paint over finished works in the pursuit of "truth." I work in dark tones: blacks, browns, grays and dirty colors. These are colors that I like aesthetically and that refer to Goya and other artists I feel close to; they also have the expressive weight needed to communicate the struggle of existence. I seek to spiritually embody human suffering in my paintings; my palette and the expressive strokes of paint are meant to convey these ideas and feelings. I feel ambivalence toward the narrative in my work—my brush strokes are intentionally somewhat clumsy. Goya, Orozco and Guston are painters I love who also use an awkward approach to paint handling. It communicates uncertainty and vulnerability; it expresses our inability to fully understand the causes and effects that shape the world.

It is in our vulnerability that something truly human expresses itself. The absence of certainty lays our souls bare; our differences become minimized as we see the inescapable truth of our shared humanity. Farr seeks to find an expression of this state of being in her paintings, to leave the noise and hubris of heroic and political declarations behind, and to hear the sound and silence of our mortality.

We spoke of Goya and of his "journalistic" approach to capturing the human condition, suffering and bloodshed. The Peninsular War gave him an abundance of tragedy to record: deeds that humans are capable of and the horrors of war. There is an aspect of his work that simply points the finger to these acts of violence. There is a moral aspect, too, but it does not make claims that any known course of action would alter these events. It is the tragic facts on the ground that Goya records, which communicate the moral dilemma of living in a body—of the fight to survive and the base animal instincts that can override our compassion and empathy. Rebecca Farr's work touches upon this, but with a distinctive spiritual dimension. Her experience of suffering is in part informed by her practice of Zen Buddhism, of sitting zazen; her vision as an artist is shaped by the spiritual acceptance that our suffering is an inescapable intrinsic reality, and that compassion and empathy are the only meaningful responses to this plight.

Her paintings are heavily worked, the scarred surfaces a record of her search—the pentimento of seeking the ineffable— the experience of "being" wrought in the greasy mixture of earth elements and seed oil. Paint has a life of its own—a soul. The limitations and possibilities are one aspect of its character. The other is a presence, a third party, that reflects something about our individual nature; it reciprocates our efforts and intentions with reflections of ourselves that are outside of our control. Farr spoke of a recent development in the conversation she is engaged in with her paintings:

I have always pushed the paint hard, painting over areas, reworking the surface, pushing the paint to wrestle something from it. I have recently felt a need expressed by the paint itself to have a lighter touch. I want to allow the paint to breathe, to be itself. I see it as a form of mercy, a relinquishing of my needs, to allow the needs of the paint to express its nature, its character. It is also a shift in my own spiritual struggle, of my personal journey.

A painting in her studio, *Newspaper 3*, uses the figure from Goya's *Third of May 1808* whose upraised hands of surrender to the firing squad communicate a plea for mercy as well as the pathos of his helplessness. In Farr's painting we look down from above, the hands emerge from thickly applied strokes of paint. The pattern of the brush strokes and the deep leaden blues give the impression of water, maybe the hands of a drowning man reaching for help. The reference to Goya informs and contextualizes the image in an ambiguous light. Another figure at the bottom of the canvas reaches toward the man. Are they swimmers enjoying the water or a person helping another whose life is in peril? We do not know. The painterly surface obscures a clear reading of their actions, the tone is dark and somewhat somber. One can read it as an immersion in water or in the chaos of unknown forces that envelop us. Our lives are governed both by our intention to act within the general torrent of history and by the capricious nature of fate. This painting has a strange poetic power. The heavily worked surface is deeply satisfying, oil paint laid on in an emotionally honest approach, its thick impasto beautifully realized. The figures exist in an uncertain way. There seems to be a struggle to survive, maybe even to survive Farr's additions and subtractions of the image. The quiver in the fingertips vibrates delicately, asserting a desire to remain: "Have mercy," they plead to the maker and destroyer of images.

In meditation one follows the breath, finding a center to disengage one's attachment to the thoughts and feelings that move like clouds in our mind. The storm of ideas, fears, impulses and desires rages in the silence. Rebecca Farr's paintings are embodiments of those thoughts and emotions. Her paintings are fearless records of a spiritual battle to find the divine in the body of suffering. She seeks to redeem a form of spiritual truth from the seeming absurdity of the human condition: this body, this planet and this universe are all finite, impermanent. Our actions give us the ability to create from a zero point something that communicates meaning. A painting is a complete universe of thought and form; it exists in the mind of the viewer, engaging and communicating filaments from another's existence. Rebecca Farr is on a spiritual and existential journey, searching for the embodiment of self in the flesh, and amidst the struggle to survive, the acceptance of our suffering as a spiritual component to being human.

Our experiences are painful and sometimes annihilating, and if we have the strength to crawl out of and excavate that wreckage, we have to ask ourselves how to describe the truth of it.

Hilton Als, *The Art of the Essay No. 3*

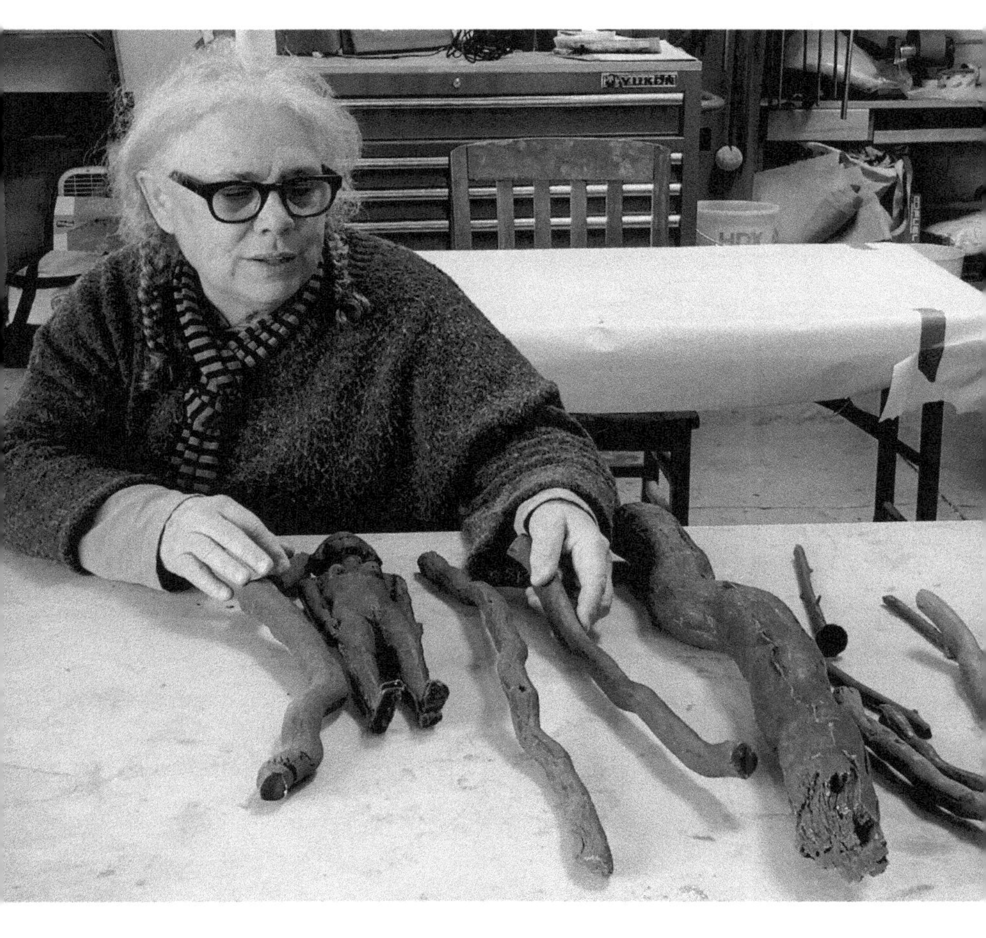

ALISON SAAR

*I Wanted to Make Art
that Told a Story*

The artist Alison Saar set a goal for herself long ago: to clearly communicate her ideas and emotions through the power of form. Her sculptures have their own personal vocabulary that speaks in a direct language about history, race, and mythology. If her sculptures are the melodies that capture one's soul, the narratives behind them are the lyrics.

Saar draws from many sources to create her sculpture, graphics and paintings; she is influenced by the art of ancient Europe, Africa, African American folk art, and German Expressionism. Primarily, though, her works tell the stories of the African American experience and these change through time as the times change. Her exhibition at LA Louver, like her earlier one there in 2016, was moving and cathartic, addressing the current political climate and how history repeats itself. Although much has changed, Saar conveys how old systems are still in place, impacting the lives of people of color.

Alison Saar grew up in a family of artists: her mother is the renowned Betye Saar, an African American artist who gained national attention for her work in the 1960s that directly addressed racism and cultural stereotypes. Alison Saar's sister, Lezley Saar, is a painter and installation artist whose work engages with the myths and fluid conceptions of both biracial and transgender identities. And her father, Richard Saar, was a ceramic artist. He also had a business for conserving art where Alison Saar worked for many years, intimately learning techniques and styles by restoring works of art ranging from ancient Chinese frescos to African sculpture.

Alison Saar was born and raised in Los Angeles. I visited her home and studio in Laurel Canyon, just a few miles from the house she grew up in, where her mother still lives. Her current home is nestled along one of the narrow, serpentine streets that traverse these magical canyons, filled with architectural jewels including several mid-century, case study homes. As I drove up she was casually dressed, having just arrived home from walking her dog. We spoke in her living room, a space filled with her art, including that of friends and family, as well as folk art that she has collected.

As a child we often visited Watts and my mother's grandmother had lived near the Watts Towers. My mother grew up while Simon Rodia was still building them," said Saar at her studio. "We also visited Grandma Prisbrey's Bottle Village and Trapper John's Old West Lodge; this work had an impact on me, influencing and shaping my vision.

While in school at Otis College of Art and Design, Saar worked with fiber art, creating works that referenced Mark Rothko and tantric art. At a certain point she realized that she wanted to create art that communicated clearly.

I wanted to make art that told a story, that would engage people. I wanted them to be moved by my work, whether it was specifically what my intentions were or not did not matter. I wanted them to be drawn in and affected by my sculpture.

For her thesis in art history at Scripps College, Saar focused on the work of self-taught African American artists such as Horace Pippin, William Edmondson, Nellie Mae Rowe, Clementine Hunter, Bill Traylor, and others. Their work, which is often spiritual and spoke directly about their life experiences, affected Saar deeply.

Ancient European art has also been influential for Saar. She is especially drawn to the Kouros, an ancient Greek sculpture of a young, naked man.

There is something in the power and force of its form. The tension between movement and stillness, she observed.

All of these influences can be felt in her sculptures, which explore the power of form to invest a work with emotional resonance.

After Saar graduated from Otis, her husband, Tom Leeser, accepted a job in digital effects in New York City, so they moved into a loft in Chelsea, long before the galleries came. At that time in the early 1980s many people were renovating their spaces in Manhattan—gutting them to make leaner, more modern interiors. Saar was drawn to the tin tiles with designs pressed into them that covered the walls and ceilings of 19th- and early 20th-century buildings. The tin tiles would become a signature element in her work, sheathing the sculptures and adorning the frames of her assemblages. She also salvaged posts and beams from the streets of Manhattan, the found materials giving her works the patina of age, the dilapidated look of time weathering and corroding our world. After living in New York for 15 years and giving birth to her two children, Saar and her family returned to Los Angeles.

Saar moves freely and seamlessly from the deeply personal to more political work, dealing with the history of race in America. She has made work that speaks of her experience of becoming a mother, creating narratives about the African deity Yemaja, a mother spirit and patron saint, especially of pregnant women. In her solo show at LA Louver, Saar addressed the history of slavery in America. The title of the exhibit, *Topsy Turvy*, is a reference to the character Topsy in *Uncle Tom's Cabin*. In the novel, the inhuman treatment that rendered her callous and indifferent to life is transformed through love, leading her to be filled with hope and a desire for good.

Saar interprets Topsy as a symbol of defiance and strength. The sculptures stand with various tools of servitude, a sickle in one and a clothing iron in another. One senses that these tools could be turned into weapons, creating a powerful emotional charge to the work. The patina of hammered metal, the tin tiles that Saar has used for years, adds an aura of melancholy pathos to these sculptures. Their tone brings to mind a quote by Zora Neale Hurston, "Grab your broom of anger and drive out the beast of fear." It is as though these words could have been written about Saar's work.

Her intimately personal, politically charged works speak of the tragic histories of racism in America that have been reawakened and made more visible in our current times of political turmoil.

Perhaps the difference between the latest body of work is that in the past my work has always viewed politics and the sword of healing approach, and I think this is the first time I've had a show that is just outright angry and maybe a little more aggressive in terms of pushing back," said Saar of "Topsy Turvy". *Often the work will look at contemporary issues through a historical lens.*

As one visitor, who was at the exhibition opening at LA Louver from the beginning to the very end, said of Saar's work, "It tells so many stories, so many histories." It is this vision that Saar had long ago: to use the power of art to tell stories, and especially ones that matter.

What is an idea? It is an image that paints itself in my brain.
Voltaire, *Philosophical Dictionary*

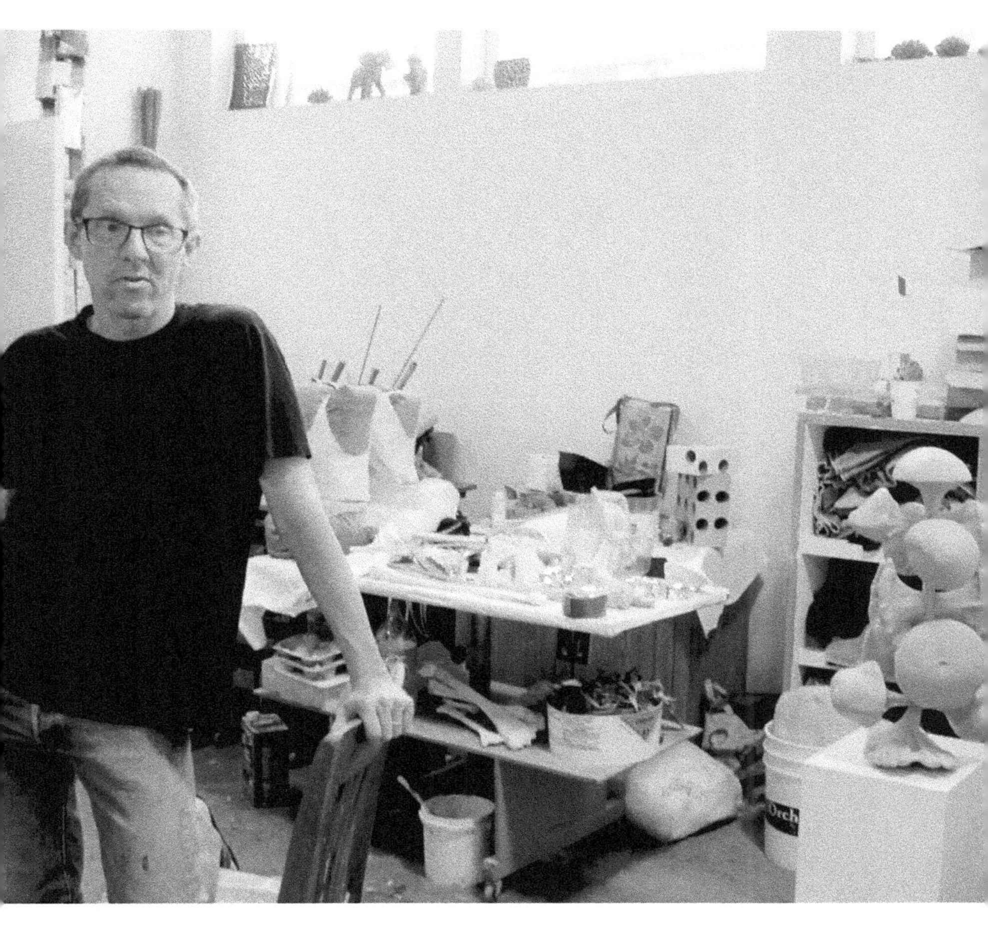

TIM HAWKINSON

The Indices of
the Unknown

Art is a philosophical quest, a method of discovery. In the right hands it can become a vehicle to seek and question the ways we think and feel. Our perceptual limitations are hidden from us. Through the lens of art we can explore the secret aspects of our bodies, our minds and the universe—the indices of the unknown.

Tim Hawkinson is a protean artist. His work is driven by ideas, an obsessive act of exploration and discovery. His art probes the space between self-perception and the hidden reaches of the body. As he told me,

> *We carry a map of what we look like and how we appear to others, but much of our bodies is hidden from our view, we cannot really know what we look like. We have these little brains that cannot quite understand the body. We cannot see much of it, but we feel confident that we know what we look like. I still feel like I am in the body of a child, but recently my daughter took a picture of my wife and I dressed up for an upscale event. When I saw the photo, I looked like my grandfather; it was a shock.*

The primal schism between what we think we know and the hard facts of reality is one of the avenues that Tim Hawkinson traverses in his varied, multitiered and imaginative approach to creation.

> *I focus on one part of the body, the rest of reality is a casualty of creation. I scavenge for odd logic, for the unexpected,* he says.

Years ago, I saw his sculpture titled "Head": it was a mold, for lack of a better term, that he had made by painting countless layers of latex on the inside of a bathroom. Sink, tub, toilet, everything was captured. He pulled it free, hung it in the middle of the gallery and inflated it. It was a remarkable object that engaged the viewer but defied immediate recognition. It took several moments to start to identify its component parts, "There is a toilet, that is a sink." Slowly one came to realize what it was. The strangeness of the revelation, and the raw power of its sculptural form, were intoxicating. Like an object from another culture or world, it held the viewer in its grasp, without our knowing what it was or what it meant. Next to it, hanging and inflated, was a latex "skin" of Tim's naked body, seemingly floating in space. When I asked about these two pieces, Tim replied,

> *It was a part of my inflatable series. I had already done my body, and the bathroom was a logical correlation; it's a room where the bodily needs are taken care of. I had no idea of what it would look like, I was just following the odd logic of the idea.*

Our senses are limited; imagination fills in the blind spots. We have a collective faith in the conceptual maps that culture, belief and our limited understanding of the universe give us. Tim Hawkinson has created works that explore the dark matter of our world. He searches and finds representations of the immaterial stuff that informs and shapes our consciousness. An idea becomes a methodology for mapping the contours of what is just out of reach, around the corner from cognition. Many years ago he created a piece called "Blind Spot" in which he photographed all the parts of his body that he could not see, and then pieced them together to create a strange map of the unknown. The result is an astonishing work. It is in the realm of the grotesque but has the innocence of a child endlessly asking questions about the world. The piece reflects an existential curiosity combined with a remarkable inventiveness to resolve the quest. It could be a map, or the hide of an unknown animal. From the anus, following the spine up the lower back and spreading wider from bottom to top, it is a continent of the unknown, the parts of the body that remain hidden to our eyes and to our closest ally: self.

When I visited Tim in his studio, he was working on a quite different piece. He was using his body to create an eccentric image of a twisting figure. The image was made by Tim standing on a base that was slowly rotating, while his wife, Patty, was taking photographs, approximately one frame every couple of seconds, about one hundred images per rotation. He then cut quarter-inch-wide horizontal strips and collaged them together, creating the appearance of a twisting figure. After he completed them, he saw that the piece had a connection to the Baldachin, the spiral pillars by Bernini over the high altar of St. Peter's Basilica in Rome. The piece looks like a digital 3-D scan of some kind. The four images of Tim's body as spiraling columns of flesh with strange distortions become slightly grotesque. The body twisting, maelstrom-like, suggests an image from Dante's Inferno, or some mythic genie emerging from a bottle. It also alludes to David Hockney's "Pearblossom Highway" and Hockney's efforts to challenge the dominance of single-point perspective. In Tim's piece he is traveling through a wormhole of form and history, the contours of his body shape-shifting into a classical masterpiece of religious art and architecture.

We spoke at length about how he "scavenges for odd logic," searching for materials that suggest ideas to explore.

One piece may lead to another, or something may come to my mind fully formed, he told me.

His studio is filled with an assortment of objects he has collected. He salvages synthetic amber, the leftover artifacts of materials that have dried in their can or bottle, left unused for too many years. Resins, enamels, mold-making materials that have solidified, have been pried from their containers and now adorn the shelves and ledges of his studio, awaiting the moment when an idea will give them formal and narrative purpose.

He has many musical instruments in his home and studio, violins as well as instruments he has made. Indeed, sound has been a component in many of his works. "Tiara," made from recycled silver-colored plastic objects, is a large tiara on a structure with a motor attached that slowly turns it round and round. In the middle are small metal tanks that once held oxygen or other gases. Hawkinson has created a musical instrument of sorts with these recycled tanks. As the piece turns, balls tumble about inside the tanks, creating soft metallic sounds, not unlike a steel drum.

The patterns never repeat; it rotates on two axes, so there is no discernible pattern. The piece is a reflection of my daughter, who is fourteen. Somehow it is about growing up and the innocence of youth.

I asked Hawkinson many questions, trying to find a frame or structure to contain the tentacle-like imagination of this protean artist who seemingly discovers his formal inventions in the blind, as it were. He finds an idea first, and then, in episodic epiphanies, each step forward reveals the formal means to give shape to his ideas. By this subjective methodology Tim arrives at remarkable sculptural objects.

As we spoke he said,

I have approached making my sculptures and images from many different ideas, using my body is just one of them. Recently I have wanted to use my body to tell stories. The piece over there is a representation of Moby Dick using my body parts to reenact the image of the whale, the ship and the men lost at sea. I am not sure of the title yet, whether I will include Moby Dick in the title or not.

The piece sat in the corner, a slightly comic handmade bathtub that could have been designed by Robert Crumb, containing casts of the knees, feet and fingers of Tim's body. Blue denim swatches from Levi's pants had been sewn together, then cut with holes to allow these elements to protrude. The Levi's are the water of the sea, a knee bent with the calf and thigh articulate the form of the great white whale, his two feet are the fluke, his fingers and hands become the ship and the men lost at sea. It is both comic and tragic, containing the pathos of the scene but with an element of comedy.

To be an artist is to reflect a spiritual truth about the creative impetus, the mysterious force that forms our world. Many faiths ascribe different stories to creation, but the state of grace that has brought into being our world and our ability to think, feel, love, remember and imagine is a mystery that art touches upon. We are part of a river of creation that has flowed through the universe from the beginning of time. To create, to care, and to bring forth the fruits of our creativity is to be an agent of this mystery.

Tim Hawkinson's work touches upon some of the deepest quandaries of self and consciousness. It does so with a scale of imagination that bends the mind to consider the unknown, with a blend of humor and pathos. His materials are common objects from the world we know, through Hawkinson's alchemy transformed into conduits of his imagination. In this act of creative transubstantiation, the world we know is renewed, and our sense of the skin we live in is transformed.

When form's in place, everything within it can be pure feeling.
Chris Kraus, *I Love Dick*

There are so many kinds of reality, and so many secret openings in the walls we think are mute.
Hélène Cixous, *Eve Escapes*

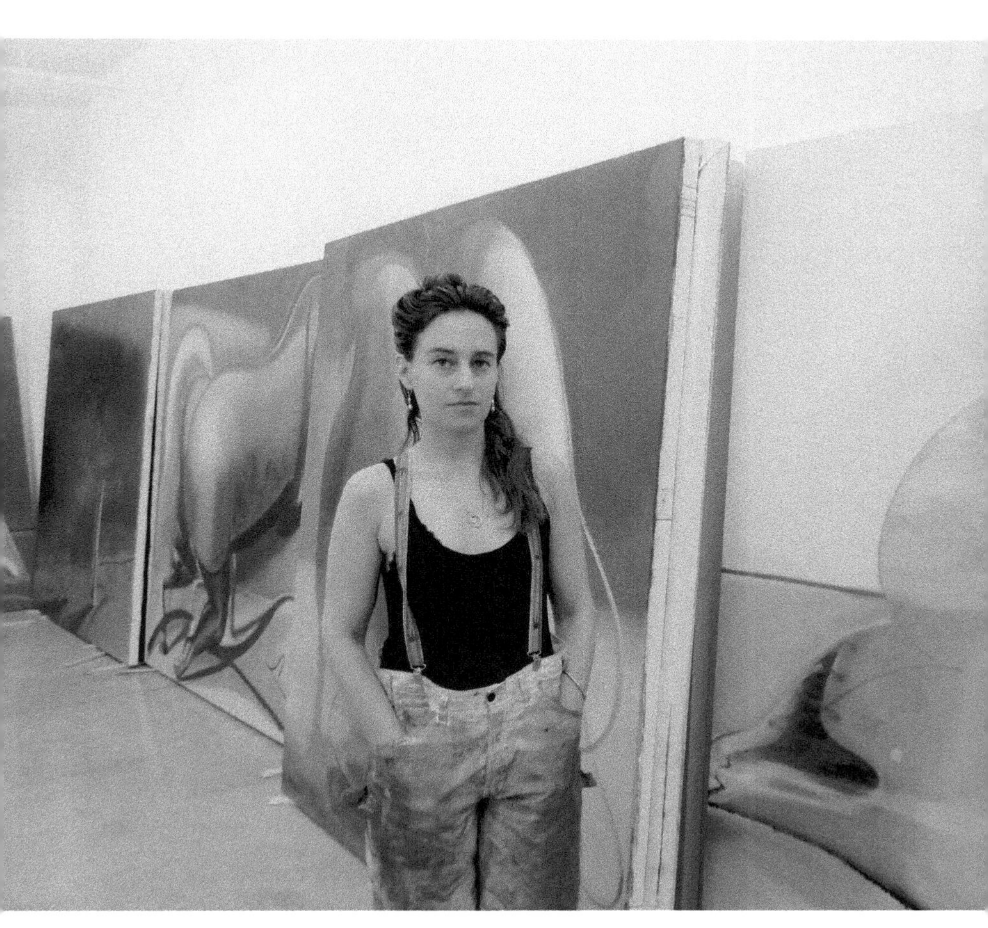

KATHERINA OLSCHBAUR

Form as Potential

Paint has the ability to create feeling: it is supple and fluid in response to the subjective states of mind that guide the painter's hand. Form exists in its potential of becoming, of transformation: it is the pregnant poetry of metamorphosis. Synthetic hybrids of abstract and figurative elements can coexist in a unified whole, forms that meld in the mind and suggest an ambiguous universe of possibilities.

Katherina Olschbaur creates lush, suggestive paintings where forms figurative and abstract elements are in fluid conversation. They are at times bold and mysterious, in others erotic and humorous; she gives herself the freedom to discover in spontaneous epiphanies the content of her imagery. Her palette is both the pigment she uses to paint bold gestural strokes of oil on canvas, and the sense impressions and memories she has collected.

I am like a sponge, I absorb things I see and I use them in my paintings. I have so many things that I have gathered in my memory, when I paint they come out of me.

We spoke about her move to Los Angeles from Vienna a little over a year ago, of how the freedom and openness of the creative world in Los Angeles has been liberating.

In Vienna the weight of history was always present, you could not get away from it, she said. *In contemporary art everything was driven by theory, I felt restricted by this pressure. In Los Angeles you can do whatever you want, there is a much more open and generous spirit. People are curious and open to different ways of creating art.*

When we first met in the Bendix Building, where we both have studios, I dropped in to see her work. She was creating essentially abstract paintings with spatially ambiguous passages that created an illusion of space, light and shadow. Hovering in an enigmatic realm, they were reminiscent of Markus Lüpertz's work of the 1980s. The spatial tension against the abstract forms was deeply satisfying and poetic; her paint was applied in bold, loose gestures that seemed casual but at times would require many applications to get the look and feel just right. Over this last year, her work has evolved to include images of shoes, horses, and fragments of the body, freely abstracted and adapted to yield to her impulses and inventions of form, space and feeling.

In her studio there was a painting in process of a shoe: the shoe is boldly in the foreground, filling the space from top to bottom, framing and cropping the background. Its high heel is suggestive of architecture, a full, sensual, curved column that anchors space and establishes a powerful figure-ground relationship. The sensuous erotic curve of the flesh-colored heel suggests the body and conveys carnal pleasure, but with a delightfully light comedic touch. The background is painted in subtle pale peaches and yellows. A serpentine line that starts at the point of the heel's contact with the bottom of the painting, moves the eye back into space. A simple and obvious device that smiles sardonically at the visual trick, but it functions to create a deep space that gives the painting breathing room and lures one into the light-filled landscape beyond.

She explains,

I have many feelings that go through my mind when I am painting. I do not control them but allow them to shift the content of my expressive touch and gesture. In one area it may feel humorous, and in another dark and anxious. I am deeply influenced by the German painters like Martin Kippenberger and Markus Lüpertz, the way that they used humor. You need to use humor to be serious. It opens up a space for one to enter a deeper place in the painting and into human consciousness.

For a solo show at Nicodim Gallery, she began a series of paintings that freely explore the poetic and narrative possibilities of the image of a horse. One senses reference to the Lipizzaner stallions of Vienna as well as an allusion to the cowboy mythologies embedded in the West. Olschbaur spoke about her fascination with the fabled identity of the cowboy.

It is an American myth of independence and self-reliance that is still a powerful metaphor in the West. This idea that one can create their identity is fascinating to me. Being from another country, I find that I create my own myths of who I am and where I come from.

The curves of the horse's body play a powerful part in her free interpretations of their anatomical forms. The bold shapes are playfully sexualized and suggest connections to Greek and Roman myths of bestiality and human/animal deities such as centaurs and satyrs. These paintings have a deeper sense of humor than any of the other works in her studio. Her statement "you need to use humor to be serious" is more evident in these paintings, where sexualizing animals plays more easily with the element of comedy; they tickle and delight, as well as shed light on the histories of our human/animal nature.

In one painting, two horses, their bodies reduced to two powerfully abstracted forms, were originally painted mirroring each other in the act of jumping. Painted in a warm sienna palette, the shapes have a formal poetry that articulates sculptural volume. Their equine shapes are coming forward in space against a luminous field of glowing yellow that transitions into a dirty, dark yellow mixed with black. The loose painterly gestures breathe freely and allow light and color to expand into deep space. There is something satisfying in the seemingly casual touch that achieves a very specific feeling. At one point in the process, the horses' bodies were altered, adapted and fused with human bodies, changed into chimeras. Olschbaur said,

I was painting the beautiful forms of the horse's flank, the shapes are so sensual and sexy, I wanted to sexualize them further, so I spontaneously and very quickly changed them into the bottom half of a human body. The shapes are very erotic. I work very fast and I painted them wet into wet, so it has this fresh feeling. When I paint, I work until the form, color and narrative become unified.

In the newest works the gestural and figurative elements have found a deeper unity. A single color fills the field, with fragments of the human body—a leg, for instance, or a torso. In another painting we see the leg of a horse and a shoe, with the suggestion of a human leg. These works have a power in the ease of the conversation between disparate elements held together simply through the unity of color. A casual black brush stroke expressing a muscular sensuality shape-shifts into a leg adorned in a costume from a 17th-century painting. They are playful, with a poetic power that beguiles in its narrative complexity, yet is accomplished through a simple, visually satisfying wholeness, allowing the images to enter one's consciousness like a vision.

Katherina Olschbaur creates chimerical paintings that synthesize form and feeling into rich vehicles of metaphoric expression. She pieces together fragments of form, gesture, memory, and figurative elements to create open-ended narratives that explore the contours of her changing thoughts, feelings and emotions. She says of her work, "I am always looking to find a way to include life into the art. I am less interested in developing a style, but more interested in finding ways to fuse all the different levels of reality—lived reality—and energy into my painting."

Painting is a profound medium. Even the word medium implies conveyance of occult knowledge, of communicating with different levels of reality. It is a form of alchemy that records the living, sensate experience of the artist, thoughts and feelings captured in matter and light. In these paintings Olschbaur adds her mark to this endeavor: each is an utterance into a luminous space, in search of an echo resonant with the energy of life.

The real voyage of discovery consists not in seeking new landscapes, but in having new eyes.
Marcel Proust, *The Prisoner: In Search of Lost Time, Vol. 5*

A medium of communication is not merely a passive conduit for the transmission of information but rather an active force in creating new social patterns and new perceptual realities.
Leonard Shlain, *The Alphabet Versus the Goddess*

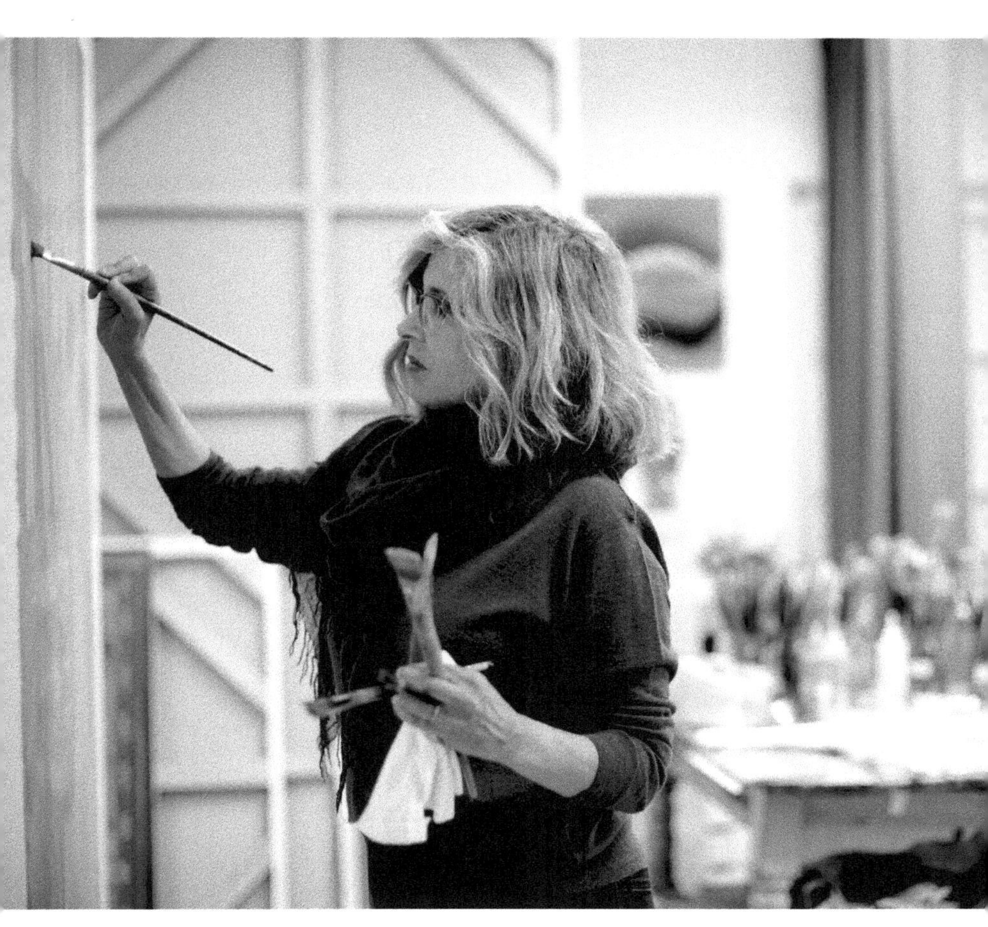

KIMBERLY BROOKS

The Metaphysical Touch

Painting is a medium that allows the artist a direct conduit to the mind, body and spirit. The perceptual sensitivity of the eye and the somatic memories embedded in the body allow one to make expressive marks that tell stories in themselves, or that shape our feelings and the way we interpret an image. The voluptuous physicality of oil paint and its sensual power to communicate feeling and ideas is unique; the immediacy of its impact conveys layers of meaning in a singular gestalt.

Memory fragments coalesce into narrative wholes; the energy of a stroke of paint communicates an emotional truth. Painting is a shorthand entrance into the soul of the maker. Kimberly Brooks uses these elements in an open process: the ideas that initially shape the direction of the painting are open to change and shape-shift in the process of creation. Memory of place, vestigial fragments and historical erasure are themes that move freely through her poetic images.

In Brooks's early work she created portraits of friends and family. The meaning of these intimate paintings was contained within the personal histories of her life, and through capturing a likeness of her subjects. They were done in a fresh, abbreviated style with an immediacy of approach similar to the work of Elizabeth Peyton. Her love of the physical medium of oil on canvas was fully present, each stroke of paint holding its own as an expressive gesture that also captured the scene and her subject.

At a certain point, the painterly qualities of gesture, and its capacity to simultaneously describe and obscure, became central to her work—how the movement of the brush can depict an image or erase it, leaving the ghost of a memory.

I started to blur my figures into the landscape or into the space that they inhabited. I realized that an empty room was a portrait or that a landscape was a portrait. I wanted to move away from the constraints of depicting someone and to allow the fragments and gestures of mark-making/image-making to communicate something more open to interpretation. My work tilted toward abstraction and the power inherent in the mark and the gesture.

Her recent paintings have a spatial ambiguity that often moves them into the realm of pure abstraction. Painterly gesture challenges the structures: in some paintings a room or a doorway or a building is depicted with a simple, almost schematic approach; it yields to the delicate, subdued palette, the low tonal contrast bringing everything to the surface. Color and the poetry of a brushstroke command the conversation—the image becomes both a vestigial memory of a place and an armature for Brooks to discover an expression contained in the pure emotional power of painting.

Brooks's use of gold and silver leaf adds to the sensual pleasure of the image, as well as confusing the spatial reading. In the sensory collapse of image, a supple fluidity of metaphor and meaning emerges. Gesture holds its own as a purely abstract form, but doubles as representation. A bold brushstroke becomes a leaf or a branch, a doorway to a building or the pattern covering the wall of an ancient church. The delicious integration of abstraction and representation at times brings to mind the complex fusion of surface and pattern, abstraction and representation, in the work of Édouard Vuillard.

The element of of metal leaf engages one as metaphor and ornament, as well as in its purely optical effects. Brooks spoke about the quality of light and the reflective surface.

I love how the gold activates the painting; it looks different when I turn the lights on in my studio or when it is just the ambient light from my studio windows. It changes as you walk past it, creating an immersive, interactive experience. It has both spiritual connotations and is beautiful for its pure sensuality.

Her work has had many incarnations. Some of the paintings

she has completed in the past are later painted over, the previous painting adding historical depth and content to the new work. The pentimento of the under-painting leaves its trace in both surface incident and in the colors coming through, affecting the color and feeling of the new work. It is a spiritual palimpsest, a diaristic and physical memory of the artist's creative journey.

Brooks spoke about a painting she was working on titled "Los Angeles."

> *I had a painting that I made several years ago, the interior of a palace. It seemed appropriate as an under-painting for this new work about Los Angeles. I love this city and I am circling back to it as one of my subjects. I have painted images from my journeys to India, Israel and other places rich in history; now I am coming home. I love the experience of painting over another painting, it allows me a jumping-off point, to interact and improvise from the colors and brush marks of the previous work. The glow of the reds from the earlier painting comes through the surface, deepening the color. The lush interior of the room now buried under this new piece, adds a metaphoric resonance for the cultural richness of Los Angeles and of all of the artists living and working here.*

The painting is done in a subdued palette of earth tones. The paint handling is loose and free. It is a suggestive image of two trees, their leaves painted in a staccato pattern, the sensual trunks moving up from the bottom with a swirl of paint at the base of one tree expressing purely abstract feelings of form and movement. A gestural suggestion of winged angels hovers among the branches, pale beige and barely defined. The painting is beautiful, existing in a deeply balanced space between pure abstraction and representation. The hovering ambiguity is pregnant with metaphor and the poetry of painting's ability to be simultaneously image and matter, body and spirit.

Kimberly Brooks seeks to find a space that is open to the currents of thought, feeling and memory coursing through her veins. She mines veins of gold and silver to bring the luster of the sun and moon into the poetry of her work. Painting is a language of the body. We make marks with the swoop of an arm or with the precise touch of our hands and fingers. These marks convey the physical memories of all we have experienced in this life as well as those that our parents and ancestors carried within them that are passed on to us.

Painting is a spiritual path of becoming. It is a means to discover oneself and create oneself simultaneously. In the work of Kimberly Brooks, currents of history, memory and metaphor shimmer brightly in the light of the present and are reflected in the subdued light of the past. She is looking for that momentary glimpse when a fragment becomes a whole, and the world is reborn anew.

Schools serve the same social function as prisons and mental institutions—to define, classify, control, and regulate people.
Michel Foucault, *Discipline and Punishment*

Despite all of our desperate, eternal attempts to separate, contain and mend, categories always leak.
Trinh T. Minh-ha, *Woman, Native, Other: Writing Postcoloniality and Feminism*

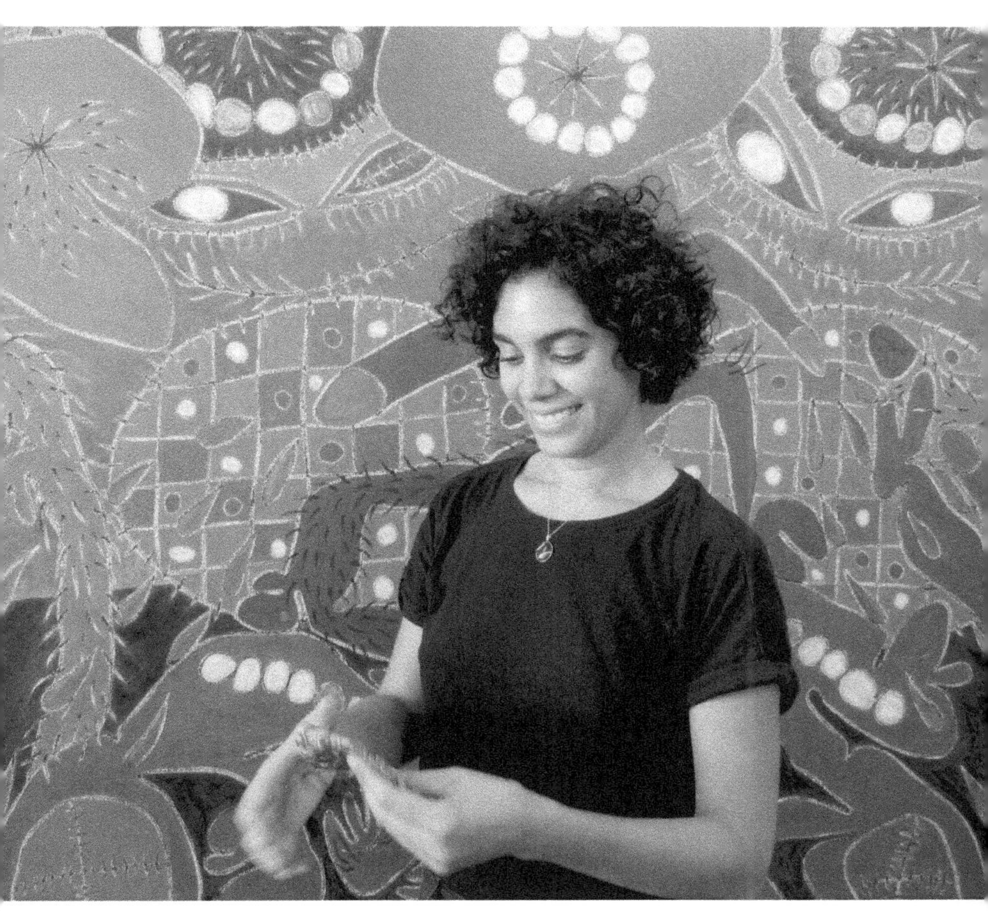

NASIM HANTEHZADEH

A Boundless Universe

The language of art is shaped by forces from within and without—history, society, and culture seek to define and control us, and our behavior is often shaped by the expectations imposed by normative modes of thought. Artistic creation can be a means to analyze and deconstruct systems of control. The supple fluidity of thought and form allows one to create images and metaphors that reflect efforts to elude these forces and to free oneself from systems of control.

Gender, race, class, religion, body type and myriad other categories become the lens through which we are perceived in the world. The subjective valuation of the "other" can be an emotional violence that defines us and places us within categories that amount to a form of oppression.

The artist Nasim Hantehzadeh's work is a form of analysis, deconstruction and rebuilding of a language that shapes content into a fluid, metaphoric, liminal space. The ideas and ethos that inform her work come from her experiences in the world. She said of herself,

> *I was born in America but raised in Iran. I returned to the United States at twenty-two and did not speak English. When I arrived as an American citizen with an American passport who did not speak English, and my looks and body language were very different than an American, I suddenly found myself in an indeterminate space. I have lived in the United States for nine years, and I even feel that "in betweenness" more intensely. For instance, if I have my family visit me in the US and I walk into a store with my mom and sister,*

we are seen as women with brown skin and an accent. It feels like that we are defined by our look, and that certain expectations shape the way people perceive us.

These are forms of definition and categorization that Hantehzadeh's work seeks to deconstruct, to create a language of fluidity that diffuses categories and maps out the subtle in-between spaces.

Hantehzadeh works in both drawing and painting. She feels that the higher economic value placed on painting over drawing is a historical bias that is arbitrary and outdated. She moves between the two and also combines them, as in the triptych she was working on in her studio when we spoke. These dualities of value become another metaphor of the space between categories for her, another element in the effort to break down definitions in her art.

She works with an intuitive and spontaneous approach, the fecundity of her imagination allowing the biomorphic forms to move freely from image to abstraction, integrating elements suggestive of viscera, male and female genitalia, orifices and eyes, in a freewheeling interplay of narrative and pure formal invention. These hybridized forms are poetic metaphors of a fluid world where categories are less defined and gender is not limited to male or female, but is non-binary and open to a world in flux, guided by the needs of the heart.

The images ricochet through history: there are suggestions of Paleolithic cave paintings, Australian and African tribal art, and surrealism as well as allusions to extraterrestrial beings. They have lightness and a weight simultaneously. Both playful and serious, they pulsate with the rhythmic cadences of the world ever-becoming, the snake shedding its skin to be renewed and a reality reborn with each shift in human consciousness.

Hantehzadeh works in large scale, the bigger pieces measuring up to 8x12 feet. The scale gives her the freedom of a fully engaged action approach. For some pieces, she uses large sticks of oil pastel on paper, applied with a loose physicality, the marks and gestures recording her hand and arm movement. She also works with oil on canvas, starting with thin washes of paint upon which oil pastels are applied. The biomorphic abstraction transitioning into figuration arises through intention and intuition, and from the interplay of memories intermingling with the present. Somatic memory and impulse flow through her mind and fingertips; in these chimerical amalgams of form and content, her imagery is a wondrous fruit culled from the rich cultural tree of human history.

Our shared world, filled with political unrest and the Coronavirus, has seeped into her work. A large triptych she worked on for months was initially titled "It smells like springtime" but was adapted to the sounds and smells of the protests just beyond her studio window in DTLA. The title is still a work in progress but became more of a narrative, pointing to the complexity of the moment: "It smells like springtime, sounds like fireworks and bullets, feels like soft bed sheets." In another piece she abstractly represents the fear and beauty experienced by a friend who gave birth during the Covid-19 plague, the anxiety of the moment mixed with the joy of begetting a new life.

When I asked her what she was doing as an artist, she responded,

> *I need to make art every day. If I don't make art for more than a day or two, I become physically sick. Making paintings and drawings is a way for me to process my emotions. When I start making work, I feel like I enter a state of mind where I can have access to my memories, but a lot of memories are shaped and reshaped by my current experiences. Sometimes the present and the current experiences are more vivid to me, other times the memories from the past become so powerful. In some pieces they merge together.*

We are shaped and defined by histories—familial, political, religious—and the genetic behavioral traits and attitudes of our ancestors, imprinted within us. Each person is an amalgam of forces that are confronted with the present, a present that is always in flux. How do we redefine ourselves and use memory and imagination to change the contours of our thoughts and beliefs—and in so doing, change the world?

Nasim Hantehzadeh seeks to create an art that reflects the interior process of her experiences in the world and her effort to dissect the modes of thought that designate and control our identities. It is a profound quest to create metaphors of a world less fixed on defining one another, to create a space where one can breathe more fully, inhale air free from the smoke of history. This is a world of beauty that exists in the heart of a poet; however, beauty is an eternal quality of mind that we seek in the physical world, this world filled with imperfection and the complexity of the human heart.

These are bold works that convey complex ideas: they express joy, anxiety, beauty and the artist's longing for a more open world, a world that allows space for each of us to inhabit. Art is a boundless universe. It is supple and fluid; indeed, the ability of a metaphor to shape-shift and retain meaning through time and place makes art a deeper form of truth than facts and definitions, which erode through time with the changes in our understanding of the world, and the shifting tides of consciousness. Hantehzadeh's ambition is a beautiful endeavor: she is mapping a world yet to become, her works are seeds for a flower still unfolding.

*When a language dies, so much more than words are lost.
Language is the dwelling place of ideas that do not exist
anywhere else. It is a prism through which to see the world.*
Robin Wall Kimmerer, *Braiding
Sweetgrass: Indigenous Wisdom, Scientific
Knowledge, and the Teachings of Plants*

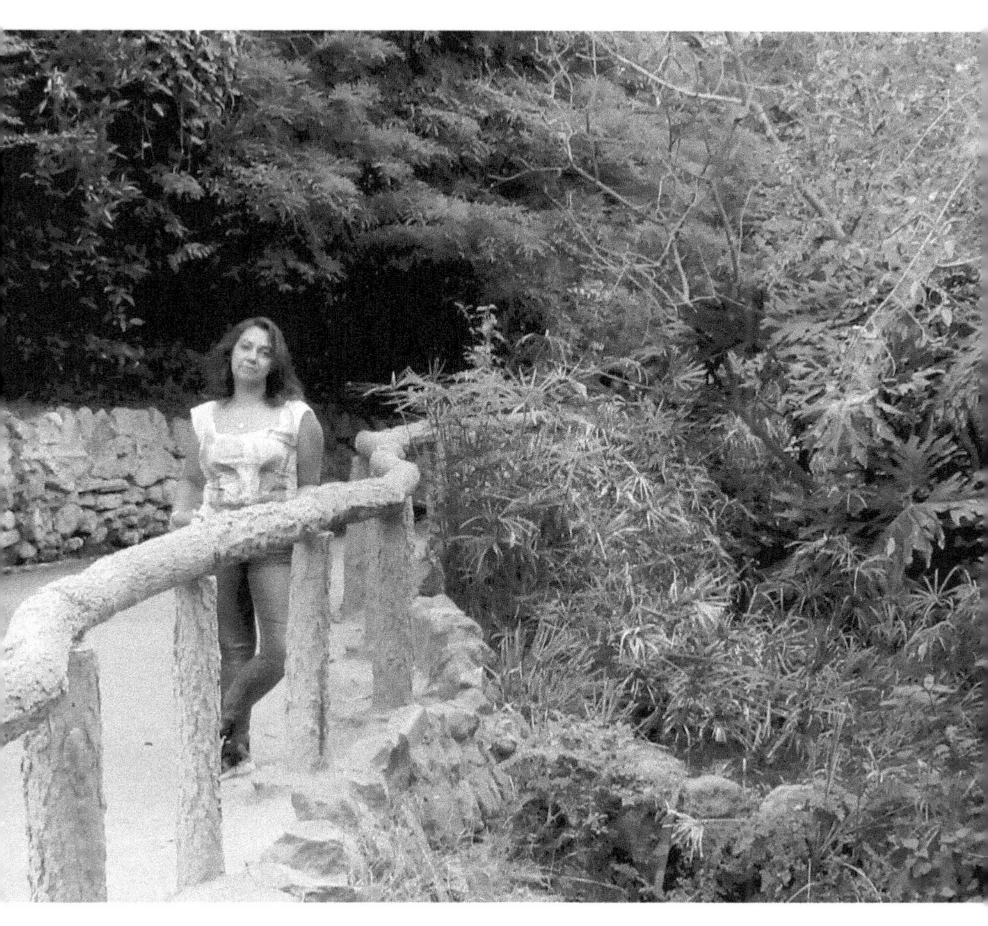

MERCEDES DORAME

In the Present Tense

An artist is a time traveler, creating worlds of ideas and emotions that will be transported into the future, felt and understood by people yet to be born. One can also make present what has been hidden, buried beneath images created by forces that shape and condition our reality. These forces attempt to erase a history and a people who are still very much alive.

The ground we walk on holds the ancestors and the stories of Native people who have been here for thousands of years, long before the arrival of Europeans. The living link to these people is here, now, just beneath the surface, in places that have been transformed into a current reality: 21st-century Los Angeles.

The artist Mecedes Dorame is a native Tongva, one of the many Indigenous groups of Southern California. In her work she reanimates the history of her people, making their living presence known through installations and photographs documenting her interventions on the landscape. Through her family history she is able to gain access to ancestral sites where she creates works in part ritual, in part a reframing of the narrative that describes her people as something from the past.

> *It always makes me angry when I see a plaque somewhere, meant to inform people of our history, that puts everything in the past tense: 'Native people used acorns as part of their diet' or 'the Tongva people used to live in this region.' We use acorns, and we live here now! My work is in part a way to transform the past tense into the present.*

Her pieces use the language of contemporary art as a means to transform the world. They assert that this is stolen land, that the people from whom it was stolen are very much alive, and that their presence must be made known and their rights to ancestral land addressed.

We met for our studio visit at the Fern Dell in Griffith Park, a natural spring that feeds a year-round creek, in an area once the site of a Tongva village. Though there is little concrete evidence there today, one can feel the presence of Native people using the water, this essential element for the life of a community. The locale is important to Dorame, as it is a place where her ancestors lived. Though she has not created a work here yet, it will be a site for a future project. She said of her practice,

> *I work outside for the most part. I create cast objects made of concrete that are representations of "cog stones," a term I dislike. I call them star stones, because they look more like stars and not like a cogwheel, as some non-Native person named them when they were first found by anthropologists. These stones are only found here and are unique to the Native people of this region. Their exact use and purpose is unknown; some see them as practical objects, but in my imagination they are ceremonial forms used for mapping celestial movement and charting pathways for moving between worlds. I use these, and abalone shells, red ochre–colored earth, and other objects that are important materials for the Tongva. I arrange them in different locations that are also important to Tongva people and photograph the installation, which I see as a collaboration with the landscape.*

I first saw Dorame's work in the "Made in LA" exhibition at the Hammer Museum. I was moved by the depth of her poetic touch, how a seemingly simple gesture could activate the heart and mind on so many different levels. She engages one in recognizing a "great amnesia" that non-Native people accept: that the land upon which we live, work, love and dream belonged just a few generations ago to people whose culture and world unfolded here over thousands of years. Her works are not a hammer or a sword, but a song that awakens a living presence. Indigenous people are here now, and their rituals and connections to this land still pulse in the hearts and minds of thousands of living souls, striving for recognition, for access to the land, for their culture to unfurl a new chapter.

In her installations, Dorame uses string to articulate a space that she said is a reference to a Yovaar, a circular structure open at the top, used by the Tongva in ceremonies connecting people to different spiritual planes.

I make reference to the Yovaar, Dorame said, but I am also thinking of light, a beam of light, starlight. I make them differently each time I create one, to respond to the environment, and the location. The star stones are placed along with abalone and different objects, and I use cinnamon to cover them. I want to connect them to the land but also the stars. I am trying to re-imagine how our people connected physically and spiritually with the night sky.

It was the installation at the Hammer that particularly caught my imagination: part painting, part object, its temporal nature giving it the metaphysical aura of a memory, of time and the elements erasing and revealing archetypal forms, thoughts and beliefs of a culture. In this piece, Dorame laid down several colors in a circle on the floor. It was outlined with cinnamon, which looks much like ground red ochre, then filled with the deepest blue of the night sky. Luminous turquoise highlights encircled star stones suggestive of the three stars of Orion's belt amid the Milky Way. Other star stones were placed thoughout the field, as well as red ochre stones and a grouping of abalone shells containing pigments or ceremonial elements. Vibrant red strings articulated a cone-like structure, rising from points around the circle and coming together, forming a space that is open, yet contains a magical universe.

In other installation works, Dorame lays down one earth pigment with the star stones placed on top, then sprinkles another pigment on top of that. Lifting and moving the stones leaves the silhouette of their shape, a memory-echo of their form. She then arranges the stones and the strings to create a symbolic image that functions as both an abstract work, whose meaning is open, and a living expression of her culture. She said of these,

I see these creations as personal ceremonies, as a way to connect with my culture and to respect and represent the presence of my people.

The string that she uses came out of her experience as a consultant. As a living descendant of the Tongva, she works at times to advise archaeologists and developers who have been called to a site where work crews constructing a road or a new building have unearthed a burial site, or artifacts from a village. Where this is happening, pottery, tools, artifacts and ancestors are unearthed by first laying out with string a grid of three-foot-square units. Carefully, a three-foot-deep hole is dug, as the archaeological team systematically sifts through the ground. At least, this is the ideal system.

When I worked as a consultant, it was a conflicted position. I would be there to advise on what they should do with the remains or objects that were found. Some would say, "Thank you. We will use your input and do our best to accommodate your suggestions." Others would just acknowledge the request but not follow the request, as there is no legal obligation to actually do anything I recommend. I felt a responsibility for my culture and my ancestors, but I also felt incredibly powerless. It is part of the reason I became an artist and what motivates my ideas and vision.

Dorame's ephemeral installations on the landscape are personal rituals: she constructs simple arrangements of string, star stones, abalone shells, red ochre and other objects used in ritual and in the daily life of the Tongva people. She documents the work in photographs.

Photography is a form of memory, she says, a way to record these private rituals and create permanent records, coding the spaces as Tongva.

The locations are places that are important to Dorame personally or to the Tongva people, and are always sites that she has temporary access to.

In one work, *To the Land of the Dead Shiishonga,* she sprinkled cinnamon onto a funnel-web spider's web, highlighting the opening, transforming it to a portal into the Earth. This subtle gesture suggests the passage into a netherworld or a spirit world. These are political and spiritual actions that use the obliquely persuasive force of poetry and metaphor to make their statement. With a metaphysical touch Dorame generates a powerful presence: past and present merge in visions that intone the song of this Earth and of the people who have lived here for millennia.

Art is a conversation through time. It reaches into the past and carries forward into the present the language of those who came before us, their visions and dreams. It is a poem written for a future whose very existence is always uncertain. This Earth and the heavens are shape-shifters, and artists are storytellers in the supple language of this ever-changing world.

Mercedes Dorame's work speaks of the concerns of Native people: to awaken the world, to say that they are here now, and that this land is still their spiritual home. Her art creates a song in the language of the stars and from the Earth beneath our feet. It is through the alchemy of art that ideas can create change, dispersed like seeds that flower, grow and transform the world.

Not everything that is faced can be changed, but nothing can be changed until it is faced.
James Baldwin, *No Name in the Street*

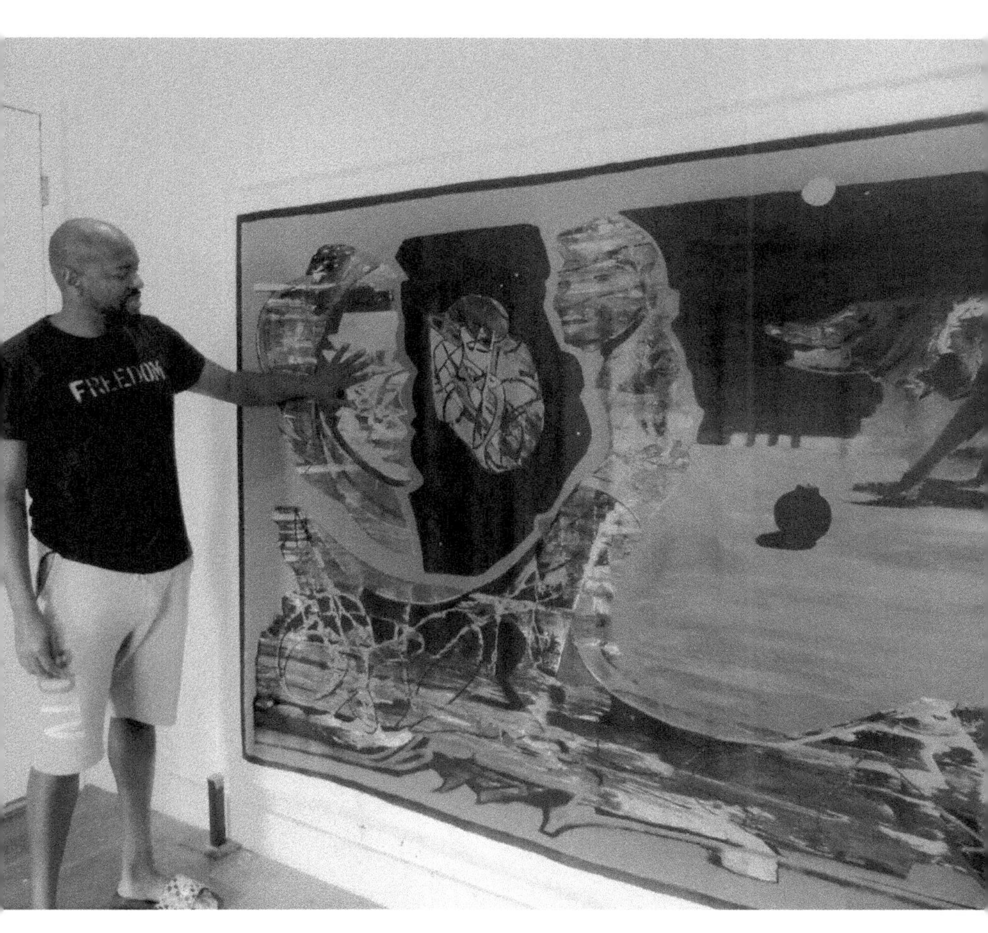

FORREST KIRK

Lightning Strikes and Other Stories

Images tell stories. An iconic image can convey layers of history and meaning. A clenched fist symbolizes unity, strength and resistance. Its use and context has reflected different causes over the years but it captures the desire for basic human rights for all.

Painting is a subtle and profound medium that expresses the spirit of the times in which an artist lives and how that artist responds to the world they inhabit. It is a nerve-sensitive medium; it records the elusive threads of an artist's subjective universe and encodes them into the matter of pigment. The surface of a painting becomes a palimpsest of the thoughts and feelings that pass through the artist's consciousness in the process of creation.

When I dropped by Forrest Kirk's studio in West Hollywood, an apartment that is within walking distance from his home, he told me that this worked well for him. He needed to be close to home to take care of his kids, and he had everything he needed if he wanted to work all night. His large paintings covered the walls, his paints and brushes occupied the floor and good natural light filled the space.

When I asked Kirk what he is trying to do with his paintings, he replied,

> *I am trying to change the world. There are many conversations that need to be had, and in my paintings I engage people with difficult subjects. I also want my paintings to be joyous—the composition and symmetry, the balance of positive and negative space, the rich surfaces and colors. But at the same time, there are many layers to my work. You can enjoy them as just a good painting or you can dig deeper. I want my*

paintings to express the joy of having a child or the sorrow of the death of your father, the hardship of losing a job and the joy I feel in painting. I think about my work like the music of Public Enemy, with Chuck D and Flavor Flav creating songs you could dance to, but when you listened carefully and went deeper into their lyrics, they were educating you—communicating the experience of black people in America and the history of racism and slavery. I want my paintings to contain all of my experiences.

Kirk has two different approaches to painting: in one he freely begins a painting with a gesture or an image without a particular narrative—just a starting point from which he can react, one mark or image suggesting another. He freely adds and subtracts along the way, leaving a rich record of the process of discovery. There is an embrace of ambiguity and a fractured narrative of images and elements that oscillate between being pure brushstrokes or gestures, and the suggestion of an image. He can find a face or a figure or some objects in a passage of pure painting, and that will lead his work in a new direction.

In another approach that he refers to as a "lightning-strike," Kirk says,

In my work I respond to what is going on around me in the world. When George Floyd was killed by the police, I responded to it by creating a series of paintings that dealt with racism and the police killings of black people. In 2020, when the coronavirus shut down the world, I had time to create some work that had been on my mind, but I had been too busy making work for different shows. I had several ideas, but the clenched fist paintings were the series I wanted to develop. I had already made a few, but I was still figuring out how to make them work. I started working on these paintings. Then the killing of George Floyd and the protests that followed happened—it really affected me deeply. It was the lightning strike, where the paintings became laser focused on this moment in time. During the protests, hundreds of people were marching down Burton Street. right outside my studio window. I had a stack of my "Fist" paintings leaning against the window, so I put one out on the balcony for the protesters coming down the street to see. When people saw it they cheered and held their clenched fists up in the air. It was a very powerful moment for me. The fist is not just about the rights of black people, but about human rights: women's rights, gay rights, and transgender rights. It is a symbol that represents all the different struggles of oppressed people.

Forrest Kirk's paintings have a raw, visceral intensity. Many of them exist in an ambiguous space, with a complex interplay of figure and ground. Silhouette-like forms act as a figure, but within them is a rich interplay of lush surface techniques: from gestural brush strokes to Gerhard Richter–like pulls of paint. The figure is simultaneously a space within which many dramas unfold. These complex interplays are a formal invention that allows the multitude of layers of meaning and narrative he is expressing to unfold in complex spaces. His backgrounds are often grays or browns, whose flat inert neutrality anchor and empower the rich painterly passages going on within the forms.

There is a deliberate naïveté to many of his images: it gives them a blunt, direct power and allows them to easily fluctuate between abstract gesture and image. Many of his paintings transmit an irrational logic that defines Kirk's approach, a kind of exquisite corpse painting, but played in solitude. Each passage leads his imagination to the next link that comes to mind: he is always influenced by events in his life and the world. He often employs a simple depiction of a bomb, which he says represents the ticking clock of time. One can also find a striped Bengal tiger wandering through these dense paintings. The tiger keeps the wild and free aspect of his consciousness alive, a reminder to stay close to the instinctual impulses that propel his paintings forward.

Other paintings are more focused on a specific subject, Kirk said about these works,

I am constantly reading, authors like James Baldwin, Maya Angelou and other black writers who speak directly to the experience of being black in America. When I read the title from Maya Angelou's book "I Know Why the Caged Bird Sings" it made me think, "What would that look like?" So I created two paintings, one with a bird and one with a cage trying to visualize those feelings. Another painting that I made was in response to James Baldwin's quote "If I am starving, you are in danger." I made an image of a husband tied to a chair in his home, with a person holding a knife to his wife's neck. When words by authors have a powerful effect on me, I want to translate those feelings into an image.

When we spoke, there was a large 6x9-foot painting titled "AfroPhysics" in the studio that he had recently completed. I asked him what he was thinking about when he made it, and he cited the recent flights into space by billionaire businessmen Jeff Bezos and Richard Branson, and simply said,

Where are the Black astronauts?

The painting is a rich assemblage of disparate elements. The use of gray to seclude various passages suggests an early Pollock painting where he would employ gray to isolate sections of spontaneous painting. In Kirk's paintings he is utilizing lateral pulls of wet paint, linear elements, swirling brushstrokes, and then out of the chaos, finding a face or a figure and adding some details to make it more discernible. A signature bomb sits in a field of blue with some kind of beast or wild animal striding through the landscape and a full moon above. The gray background's inert chromatic quality is a counterpoint to the action taking place within each distinct island of emotions and ideas. This is a very complex painting. In the artist's masterful approach, he is able to resolve the friction of these contrasting elements into a singular gestalt. It is a metaphor of seeking to face the challenges of being in our world and striving to transform it through his art.

These are important paintings that communicate on multiple levels simultaneously. They fluidly shift from the pure sensual pleasure of painting to emotionally and psychologically complex works. Forrest Kirk's ambiguous narratives pull one deeper into a personal language, a diaristic approach that speaks directly from the heart. These records of his experiences are filled with the tragic realities of racism and the history of slavery but move forward into the power of creativity to shape a new future. It is a future he strives to create through his ambition to make paintings that can change the world.

First of all I express sincerity. There's also that sense of humor, by which people sometimes learn to laugh about themselves. I mean, the situation is so serious that the people could go crazy because of it. They need to smile and realize how ridiculous everything is.

Sun Ra, *This planet is doomed: the science fiction poetry of Sun Ra*

The written history of the world is largely a history of warfare, because the states within which we live came into existence largely through conquest, civil strife, or struggles for independence.

John Keegan, *A History of Warfare*

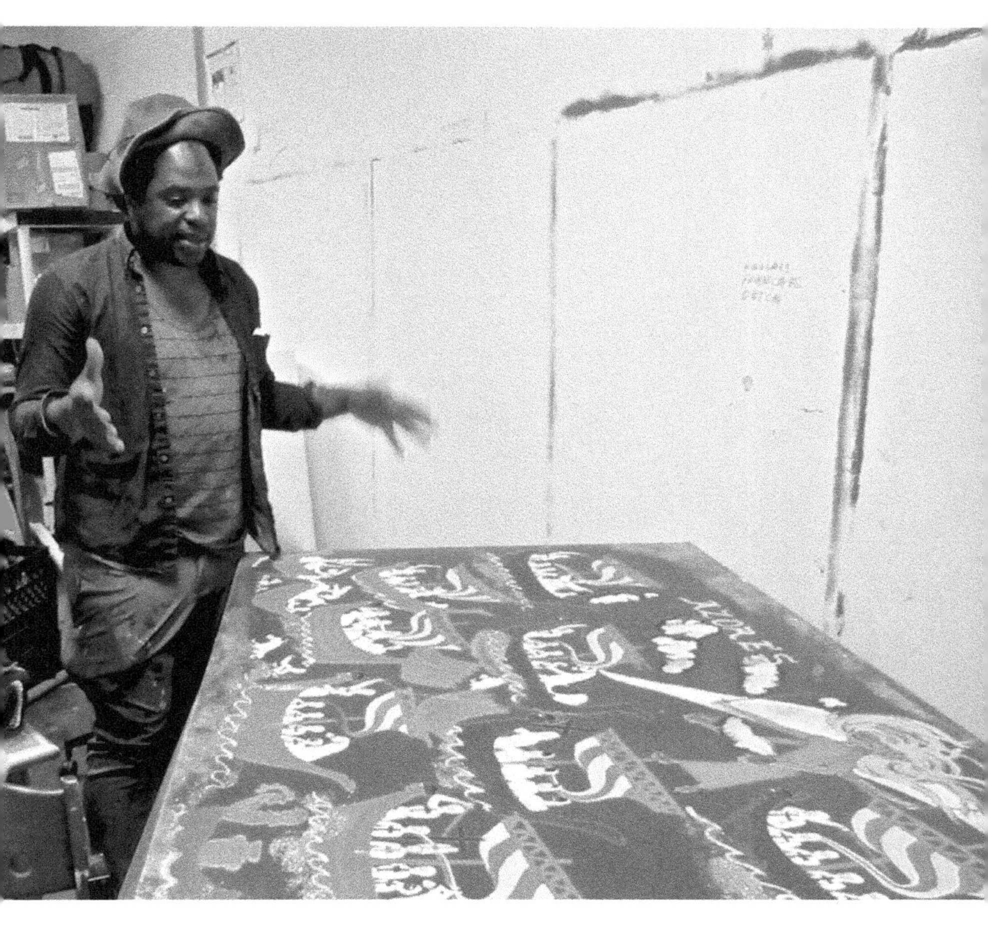

UMAR RASHID

*Meta-Narratives and the
Search for Cosmic Justice*

Humor is a key that opens the door to our shared humanity. It is a quality of human consciousness that can help us find a space to communicate about painful, difficult subjects. To transcend the cycles of violence that have shaped our world we need the influence of a trickster—Anansi, Hermes, or a heyokha—who can reveal the ways human folly shackles us to patterns of action and reaction.

Umar Rashid has an encyclopedic knowledge of history: especially the history of colonialism. He uses images of cultures through time and space to create narrative works that seek to rewrite the histories of the oppressor and the oppressed. Despite the moral weight of his subject matter, there is a humor at play that reflects his humanity and joie de vivre.

We met at his studio, where he was working on a wooden sculpture, chipping away with a mallet and chisel as we spoke. His studio was filled with works in progress and the clutter of materials he uses to creates his art. Rashid's presence exudes a warmth and generosity of spirit. To talk with him is to open the floodgates of a deep reservoir of knowledge, and as the waters cut through the historical landscape, layers of history are revealed like geological strata of time. His words come in a swift flow, punctuated with laughter and sorrow. Pausing here and there, forefinger on his chin, eyes looking up, he searches his memory to pinpoint a date: "The first rapid-firing gun, the clip gun, was first used during the Franco-Prussian War in, was that 1870 or 1871?" From these swift-flowing thoughts he creates energetic, complex compositions where histories collide and are rewritten, equal parts comedy and tragedy.

Asked about his work and intention, he said,

I create narrative paintings that have a meta-narrative and a meta-meta narrative beyond that. In my work I use humor and bright, colorful, dynamic compositions to hold people's attention and engage them in a discussion about the history of colonialism and oppression, as a way to help create change and movement in the world. How can we undo all of this anger? We do it by creating space where we can have a conversation. Our reactions can give ideas more energy, and make them more corporeal. I use humor to open up lines of communication. Racism, capitalism, colonialism, and oppressive religions—these are all just systems. These are not permanent realities—nothing is permanent. It is all a flow, and we have to work to change these systems. I was in Arizona a few years ago doing a talk and a performance. A white woman in the audience asked a question that was based on her ignorance of the history of Black people in Arizona. I corrected her by educating her about a history she was unaware of. When she sat down, the audience applauded me, and I said, "Don't do that, you are shaming her. She made a mistake, she did not know and now she does." I feel that all of this anger separates us. In my work, I try to engage people in a conversation and use humor to create a space in between the tension of opposites, and in this space a conversation can take place.

To have a conversation with Rashid is to be entertained. He speaks through his body, animating his words with a comedic physicality. He is a scholar, an educator, an artist and a jester imbuing the world with a radiant cosmic smile. There is a shamanic aspect to his work; he invokes the trickster whose antics force change in the world.

In the past, he pointed out, *rulers had jesters in their court, to remind them of just how ridiculous this all is. That nothing is permanent. Our world suffers in part because people try to hold on to ideas and systems as though they are permanent. We need more jesters in our world.*

Like his spoken words that ricochet freely through history's myriad cultures and empires that have risen to impossible heights and then fallen like Ozymandias, Rashid's paintings, drawings, appliqué, and sculptures move in a quicksilver stream through time. There is a stylistic quality of folk art to his imagery, sometimes a nod to Basquiat. A work such as "The Battle of Memphis" gives us a flood of competing symbols: Egyptian, Greek and Paleolithic figures, colonial soldiers, horses, camels, and words such as "MISSISSIPPI-MOABITE-PRAY-EXECUTE." The graphic energy and conceptual cadence come at you in a flood. Rashid has said of his work,

My paintings are filled with information. Every time you look at my work you will see something different.

His art is strewn with graveyards and gardens. Graveyards of the dead ideas that fuel the ideologies he is trying to transform, and the gardens of his imagination, where cosmic justice prevails and people free themselves from destructive patterns of behavior. A drum he made is adorned with the words "TO ALL THE PEOPLE OF THE UNIVERSE YEAH IT'S YOURS."

When we spoke, there were three paintings that Rashid had just completed on a wall in his studio. The backgrounds are lush atmospheric passages, wet-into-wet flows of acrylic paint. On their own, the backgrounds could be complete color field abstractions, creating a nebulous landscape or a cosmic space where everything-everywhere, present, past, and future are all one. In a piece titled "Bound 6 (After Kanye). Traveling the Orinoco delta. The jungle is on fire but there's always time for a toast," a Black man dressed as a colonial officer in full military regalia rides horseback; an aristocratic white woman in an ornate dress rides on the horse with him. They each hold a red 'solo cup' from our time period; an indigenous Tapir man stands nearby, also holding a 'solo cup.' Though the narrative is one of tragedy and hardship, it is delivered with absurdist humor.

We spoke about these reversals of history: inverting the power dynamic becomes a form of catharsis, an exorcism of the history of European colonialism and other empires of oppression. These inversions also speak to the capricious nature of the machinations of history.

Through history these cycles of violence repeat, he says. *Often, as one dominant power is overthrown, those who were the oppressed become the oppressor. I am trying to find a space in between those two forces—a cosmic space that transcends*

those cycles, where spiritual freedom exists. I feel deeply for people who are suffering. It affects me, and my work often develops in response to it. I feel for all people, not just my tribe but people of every race and culture. [...] It is a form of catharsis to transform that pain into these paintings filled with humor and vibrant life.

Through paradox and parables, Umar Rashid holds up a mirror to our world. His paintings engage us with a rapid-fire patter of narratives, ideas, and histories, tragicomic images that express pathos through a heart big enough to contain multitudes.

During our long, expansive conversation, Umar was working away on his sculpture, trying to carve through the block of wood to create an opening—a space. As our conversation came to an end, his chisel finally pierced the block. He slid his fingers through the opening and said with joy,

I cannot tell you how good it feels to make it through to the other side.

The random, the unscreened, allows you to find what you don't know you are looking for, and you don't know a place until it surprises you.
>   Rebecca Solnit, *Wanderlust: A History of Walking*

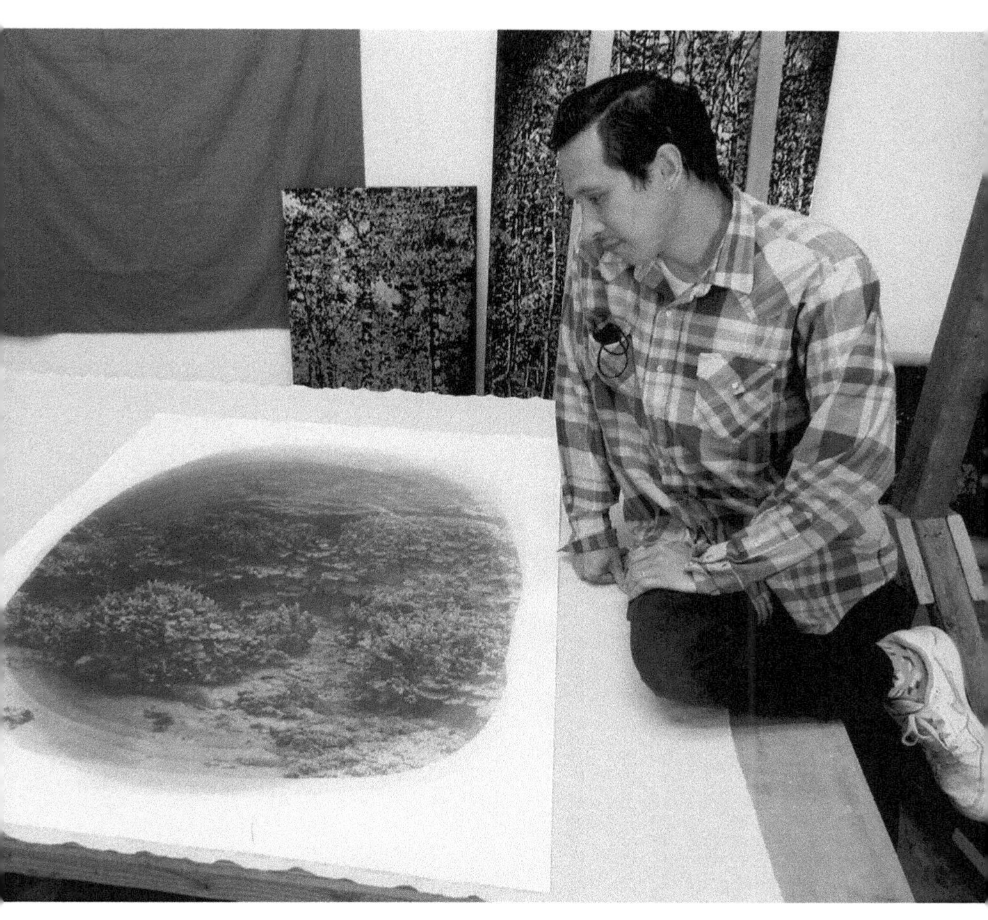

MATTHEW BRANDT

Light & Matter

I visited Matthew Brandt at his vast studio, a former carpet warehouse, in West Adams, Los Angeles. It was filled with a rich array of tools: blowtorches, a kiln for melting glass, large tubs for processing photographs, and worktables covered with various projects still in development. Outside, in the back, is a small stand-alone shed where he uses the more dangerous substances for his novel methods of creating his work, including pieces that use uranium!

Though photography is his medium, he pushes the materials and chemical techniques he employs into the realm of alchemy. His works are about process, discovery and serendipity; happenstance and location can become poetic elements in his lush metamorphic images.

As the camera captures a moment in time, the medium he uses often comes from the places where his art takes him, becoming another record: a diary of Brandt's life as a creator. Through an exhibition in St. Petersburg, Russia, Brandt learned about the significance of the birch tree as part of local cultural identity and connection to the land. He took hundreds of photographs of birch forests, which later became a series of laser-etched images on birchwood: part of the wood burned black with a laser, other portions gold-leafed, creating a poetic chiaroscuro of lightness and dark, destruction and radiance. A large, powerful piece from this series, *Birch SPDO1A,* became part of the exhibition *Light & Matter,* a 15-year survey of the artist's work.

When I asked Brandt about his work and its meaning, he replied,

When I first learned about the rich history of photography and the brilliant minds that discovered the varied chemical processes that were created to print photographs, I wanted to find a way to highlight the beauty of these techniques. I found that by throwing a monkey wrench into the process, I could reveal the rich chemical layers and alchemy behind the medium—destruction is an important part of my creative process. My works are metaphors about the unfixed, transient nature of life: that this is all a temporal moment in time. There is a Buddhist sense to these works in their expression of impermanence.

The exhibition *Light & Matter* revealed his endlessly inventive approach to creating an image. A grid of 24 photographs from his *Lakes and Reservoirs* series is a beautiful expression of his aesthetic and philosophical goals. Each piece is a four-color print. He placed each image face down in a pan of water collected from the lake; the bleeding and separating of the magenta, cyan, yellow and black create lush, dream-like colorscapes that show us the beauty of these inks as they dissipate from a fixed image to become abstract watercolors. The aesthetic accidents all take place outside the artist's control. In many of the images, an air pocket, caused by the paper bubbling, leaves an area untouched, showing a clear image of the lake and surrounding landscape. There is an innocence to these imaginative and playful experiments: as though a child, head buried in the grass, is peering through the blades of grass at the partial views of the world beyond. These are a quicksilver gaze—an alchemist squinting into the phenomenal world through a looking glass, to see what it looks like upside down.

When we spoke, Brandt mentioned that part of his practice is to include site-specific elements to his images, incorporating things he discovered from the various shows he has had throughout the world. Serendipity graces this exhibition, with a sad and humorous backstory for one of his pieces.

After the exhibition was scheduled in 2020, and I was beginning to piece together the work that would be in the show. I read an article about a seventeen-foot tall marble replica of Michelangelo's "David" that the Forest Lawn Cemetery owns. It had collapsed under its own weight, and broke into pieces. I called the museum and asked if I could photograph it and get a piece of the marble to grind into marble dust to use as a printing medium. They gave me the OK and I came with my camera. A crew with a forklift helped me move the pieces around into a composition that worked. The chunk of marble was ground to dust, and using silkscreen, I created this work, "David 1B."

The image has a ghostly presence: the marble dust, printed on roofing paper, creates a subtle, spectral image; the visage of the head, the various body parts of the sculpture feel like an apparition. The work conveys a sense of time, gravity, and the slow erosion of this world back to the dust from whence we all came.

Despite the fact that modern chemistry and science are crucial to photography, in the hands and vision of Brandt, the medium retains a deep connection to the four primal elements and conveys a sense of magic and alchemy. Water, air, fire and earth play prominently in many of the works' creation: earth as the marble dust of *David 1B*, water as a transformative agent in *Lakes and Reservoirs*, air and fire in his burnt, laser-etched images of birch forests.

For a giant diptych of glaciers in the exhibition, *Vantajökull MYCD1*, the artist used a blowtorch to heat and transform the image. The materiality of the paper and print medium becomes a rich, bubbling, abstract surface, where kaleidoscopic chromatic and tactile dramas play out in a series of lush passages. The image is obscured, transformed into a metaphor about our world, its impermanence and its continual death and rebirth. These transformations take place both from natural causes and, in our current world, man-made ones. The image of the glaciers—the surface of the photograph's pigments melted by the heat of the flame—could be seen as a metaphor of global warming, yet another reminder of our vulnerability. Our world is an ever-changing environment of violent disruptions: the strata of the Earth itself form a geological record of the endless transformations that have come before us and will continue after our time.

During our conversation, Brandt said,

My work is about experimentation and process. I do not know what the results will look like, and many times they fail. When I arrive at an image that works—when all of the

*work and the not knowing what will happen are over—I
am done with the project. I do not want to make a product.
The results that I arrive at are a record of the journey. That
is what I am after.*

Matthew Brandt captures not just the image that his camera
records. His works are a diary of a creative soul expanding the
limits of a medium to capture elements of his life and express
the ineffable space between being and nothingness. His images
are spectral and dream-like. They are a scrim through which we
perceive the world we know and the forces of transformation, the
active elements of metamorphosis. He leaves us a trace: the strata
of his experiments and discoveries, mapping the trajectory of his
imagination.

I abandon myself to the fever of dreams, in search of new laws.

Antonin Artaud, *Artaud Anthology*

For beauty is nothing but the beginning of terror, which we are barely able to endure.

Rainer Maria Rilke, *Duino Elegies*

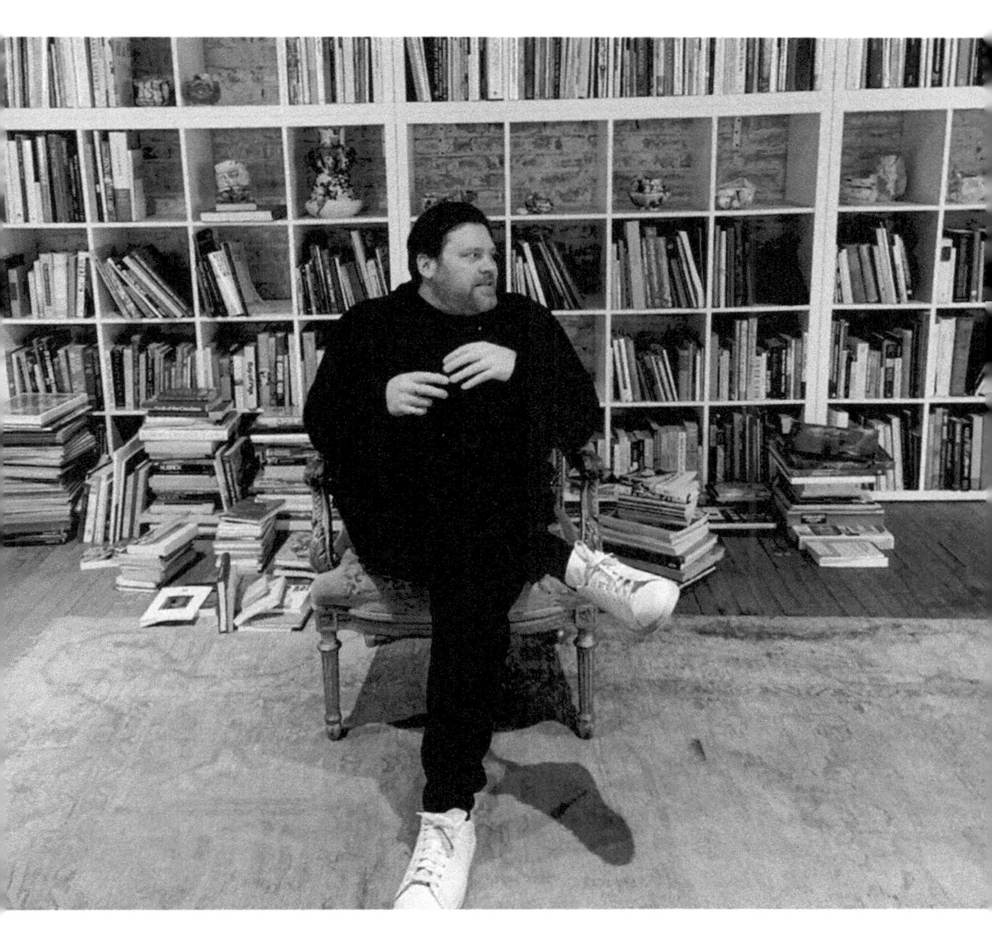

ELLIOTT HUNDLEY

Echo

The 20-year survey of Elliott Hundley's career at Regen Projects titled *Echo* was an intoxicating, voluptuous visual feast. His obsessive works filled the gallery spaces, creating an immersive installation that enraptured the mind and the senses.

Literary references to Euripides, Rilke, Artaud, and Genet are a metaphoric structure upon which he often creates. The stories and the characters in them are not only a method to give subjective shape to his work, but they are also reflections of himself, archetypal actors from our collective unconscious who have helped Hundley create his sense of identity:

> *Life is extremely complex. There are so many unanswerable questions. The obsessive collages of images in my art are an effort to feel at ease with the anxiety of existence. The tragedies of Euripides express our experience and terror of the unknown. Through catharsis, his plays are a psychological method to find some kind of peace within this reality. In my work, I am building a nest made with myriad fragments from narratives that convey the incomprehensibility of life. It is a form of catharsis and has been a way to build my identity through these stories.*

His studio is vast: a 1907 industrial brick warehouse with enormous wooden beams, weathered sliding doors, and a huge freight elevator; the brick walls exposed through layers of paint give his space an aura of history, a sublime patina of time. The building has passed through many hands and businesses. Hundley found it in disrepair, the floors collapsed and infested with rats. Nevertheless, he fell in love with this dilapidated shipwreck and resurrected it, creating a space large enough to house his dreams. It is Hundley's own Merzbau; he refers to it as his ark. The building itself is intertwined with the art that he creates within its walls. It is a nest and an inspiration. The record of the past embedded in the studio's worn surfaces exudes a reassuring warmth.

The warehouse district where he lives is changing. There are plans to build a station for a sky gondola in the lot next door to carry people to Dodger Stadium. He can see the trains passing by as they leave Union Station, and just up the street in Chinatown is the light rail station playfully adorned with architectural and ornamental elements reflecting Asian culture. Hundley spoke about these changes:

> *I love having a community. I have two spaces in my studio where I give friends and artists whose work I admire exhibitions. Right outside my window I can see downtown Los Angeles. I hear the trains as they are passing by and I can watch the firework displays above Dodger Stadium. I love the thought of a gondola carrying people up to the ballpark as they look out over Chinatown below. It is like a child's dream. My neighborhood is becoming a perfect Legoland world.*

The exhibition was a stunning tour de force of planning and installation. I had assumed the work went into the space with a general plan, combined with an organic spilling forth from one area to another. But there was a scale model of the galleries at Regen Projects in Hundley's studio with maquettes of every piece in the show thoughtfully placed.

An ecstatic Dionysian energy pervaded the show. The experience was a sensorial overload mixed with awe, blurring the boundaries between image, object and installation. Many of the artist's works are an accumulation of hundreds of small cutout photographs and collage elements pinned to the surface. From afar they engage our vision as two-dimensional works, but up close one can see that they are physically occupying a shallow space with a galaxy of images floating just inches off the surface of the canvas or panel. His collections of subject matter are not unlike insects pinned in a specimen case. Indeed, one might say that in his art there is an element of collecting and categorizing experiences, memories and stories. His works are curiosity cabinets of the human psyche, autobiographical and emotionally cathartic; myths and stories exhibited as representations of states of consciousness. His no-holds-barred approach of "more is more" is an assault against a minimalist aesthetic of economy and reductivism.

Hundley spoke about the subjective blur that exists between things.

In the installation, I used thousands of pins with small pieces of colored shapes pinned to the wall to create transitions linking one artwork to the next. I wanted to blur the physical boundaries and suggest that my works flow from one into another. The physical edges do not contain the content of my work.

He uses excess as a representation of the impossibility of completely understanding anything. Our ability to comprehend our experiences is limited by our five senses and our consciousness. Insects, birds and amphibians can see chromatic wavelengths invisible to us and can sense changes in the Earth's magnetic fields to help them navigate. We can comprehend only a limited sensory universe. Our understanding of one another is a mystery unto itself.

We can never really know another person, Hundley observed. *People we once thought we knew change and become someone else.*

"The Plague" is a monumental piece that subtly suggests Bosch's "Garden of Earthly Delights." There are shapes that echo elements of Bosch's meditation on divinity, life, death and damnation as well as a sense of a foreground, middle ground and background that implies a landscape. The myriad images coalesce into a Grand Guignol of phantasmagoria. Images of soldiers carrying the wounded from the Vietnam War; mouths and lips, fruits and other food products cut from vintage ads; surgeons operating and women dancing: a riot of life in its infinite complexity fills the surface. At the upper right is a painted Japanese theater mask. Above that is an image of a kitchen sink with gestural brushstrokes surrounding and dancing around the chrome drain, giving the impression of a monstrous Cyclops peering out from the tumult.

The title of "The Plague" refers to Antonin Artaud's play *There Is No More Firmament*. A passage from the text mirrors the actions taking place in the artwork. "A woman waves her arms, a man falls, another with his nose in the air as if scenting; a dwarf, now downstage, runs about light as a feather. A hysterical woman wails, makes as if to undress. A child cries with huge, terrible sobs." Excess is an aesthetic and philosophical choice. It is a means to capture the silent scream of life in an imagist torrent of emotion and spectacle.

The gallery became a theater of his imagination. The sculptures, paintings and collages combined with objects from his collection of artifacts shared a subjective resonance. Hundley is an intellectually curious omnivore, and his instinct guides him into the shadowlands at the edge of knowing. He sees in the tragedies of Euripides an expression of the terror that speaks to us today about the same unease we feel from the darkness that surrounds us.

How do we make sense of the world? We are all translators taking in information through our perceptions, organizing it consistent with our beliefs. The translation of words and ideas into images is central to Hundley's art. Six months ago he adopted a twenty-year-old parrot named Echo. As the Regen Project show approached, they were just getting to know each other—the interspecies translation of language that was unfolding between them inspired the title of the exhibition. In Hundley's efforts to commune with his parrot, the blur between animal and human consciousness added another element to his poetic inquiry into the unknown.

The artworks are beautiful and intoxicating. They are ornate amalgamations of "everything everywhere all at once." His approach is primordial and instinctive. With mastery and abandon he releases into his work an avalanche of information to a symphonic crescendo. This collective stream of consciousness flows from antiquity to the present, and these sibylline spectacles are a key to unlocking the doors of the imagination.

Acknowledgments

I would like to thank several people who have supported me as a writer.

First my wife, the artist Aline Mare, who is my first reader and whose sensitive insights and suggestions always help to push me further and deeper into the heart of the writing.

I would also like to acknowledge Elizabeth Bell and Pamela Barr, both editors who added their insight and expertise to the book.

Thank you to Griffith Moon publishing, for supporting this project and recognizing the importance of my writing.

And to the city of Los Angeles for its dynamic cultural life and the generosity of spirit that is shared among its community of creative artists, and the one hundred and fifty artists who I have written about in articles and catalogues essays.

My book is a reflection of this historic moment, as Los Angeles emerges as one of the major international centers of contemporary art. This book contains a fraction of the artists that I have interviewed, but with luck this may be the first of several books to come!

Gary Brewer
Los Angeles

Quotations

Preface
Wright, Frank Lloyd, *Frank Lloyd Wright on Architecture, Nature, and the Human Spirit: A Collection of Quotations,* (Pomegranate, 2011)
Foreword
Hooks, Bell, *Altars of Sacrifice: Re-membering Basquiat,* (Art in America, 1992)
Reinhardt, Ad, *Art-as-Art Dogma,* (Manuscript, 1964)
Iva Gueorguieva
Foucault, Michel, *The Foucault Reader,* (Pantheon Books, 1984)
Solnit, Rebecca, *A Field Guide to Getting Lost,* (Penguin Books, 2006)
Paul Paiement
Pollan, Michael, *The Botany of Desire: A Plants Eye View of the World,* (Random House Trade Paperbacks, 2002)
Friedberg, Anne, *The Virtual Window: From Alberti to Microsoft ,*(MIT Press, 2009)
Simphiwe Ndzube
Kafka, Franz, *The Castle,* (Schocken Books, 1974)
Fugard, Athol, *Notebooks 1960/1977*, (Farber and Farber, 1983)
Rebecca Farr
Solnit, Rebecca, *The Faraway Nearby,* (Penguin Books, 2014)
Alison Saar
Als, Hilton, *The Art of the Essay No. 3,* (Paris Review, Summer 2018)
Hurston, Zora Neale, *Dust Tracks on a Road: A Memoir,* (Armistad, 2010)
Tim Hawkinson
Voltaire, *Philosophical Dictionary,* (Basic Books, 1962)
Katherina Olschbaur
Kraus, Chris, *I Love Dick,* [Semiotext(e), 2006]
Cixous, Hélène, *Eve Escapes,* (Polity, 2012)

Kimberly Brooks

Proust, Marcel, *The Prisoner: In Search of Lost Time, Vol. 5* (Penguin Classics Deluxe, 2019)

Shlain, Leonard, *The Alphabet vs the Goddess,* (Penguin Books, 1999)

Nasim Hantehzadeh

Foucault, Michel, *Discipline and Punishment: The Birth of the Prison,* (Vintage Books, 1995)

Minh-ha, Trinh T., *Woman, Native, Other: Writing Postcoloniality and Feminism,* (Indiana University Press, 2009)

Mercedes Dorame

Kimmerer, Robin Wall, *Braiding Sweetgrass: Indigenous Wisdom, Scientific Knowledge, and the Teachings of Plants,* (Milkweed Editions, 2015)

Forrest Kirk

Baldwin, James, *No Name in the Street,* (Library of America, 1998)

Umar Rashid

Ra, Sun, *This planet is doomed: the science fiction poetry of Sun Ra,* (Kick Books, 2011)

Keegan, John, A History of Warfare, (Knopf Publishing Group, 1993)

Matthew Brandt

Solnit, Rebecca, *Wanderlust: A History of Walking,* (Penguin Books, 2001)

Elliott Hundley

Artaud, Antonin, *Artaud Anthology,* (City Lights Books, 2001)

Rilke, Rainer Marie, *Duino Elegies,* (North Point Press, 2000)

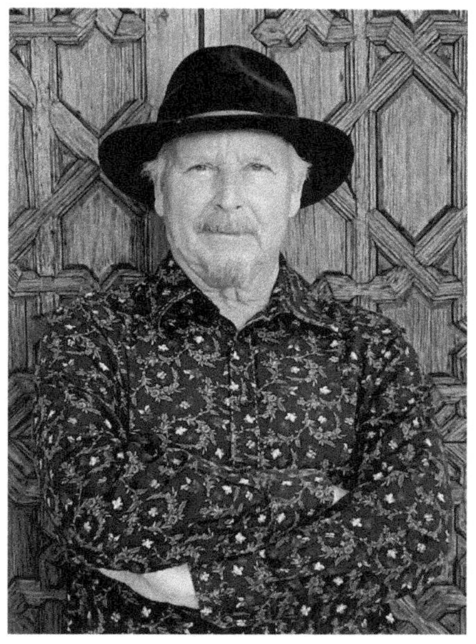

Gary Brewer is a painter, sculptor, writer and curator. His essays and interviews have been published in *Whitehot Magazine*, *Hyperallergic*, and *Art and Cake*. Recent articles include an in depth essay on the exhibition, *Clyfford Still: Dialogue and Defiance*, at the Clyfford Still Museum, Denver CO, 2024. Curatorial projects include *Vibrant Matter-Brilliant Fire: Mind, Matter, Imagination*, 2024, Wonzimer Gallery, LA, CA; *The Shape of Life*, 2021, Wonzimer Gallery, LA, CA; *Woven Threads: The Migration of Myths and Metaphors*, 2020, Brandstater Gallery, Riverside, CA. Brewer's paintings are exhibited internationally and he is represented by Wonzimer Gallery in Los Angeles, CA. He lives in Pasadena, CA, with his wife, the artist Aline Mare and their cat, Yogi.